Early Kings of Norway

Thomas Carlyle

Table of Contents

Early Kings of Norway..1

Thomas Carlyle..1

CHAPTER I. HARALD HAARFAGR..1

CHAPTER II. ERIC BLOOD–AXE AND BROTHERS....................5

CHAPTER III. HAKON THE GOOD...7

CHAPTER IV. HARALD GREYFELL AND BROTHERS..............11

CHAPTER V. HAKON JARL...14

CHAPTER VI. OLAF TRYGGVESON...18

CHAPTER VII. REIGN OF OLAF TRYGGVESON.........................21

CHAPTER VIII. JARLS ERIC AND SVEIN......................................33

CHAPTER IX. KING OLAF THE THICK–SET'S VIKING DAYS.....37

CHAPTER X. REIGN OF KING OLAF THE SAINT........................43

CHAPTER XI. MAGNUS THE GOOD AND OTHERS....................61

CHAPTER XII. OLAF THE TRANQUIL, MAGNUS BAREFOOT, AND
SIGURD THE CRUSADER...69

CHAPTER XIII. MAGNUS THE BLIND, HARALD GYLLE, AND
MUTUAL EXTINCTION OF THE HAARFAGRS............................73

CHAPTER XIV. SVERRIR AND DESCENDANTS, TO HAKON THE
OLD...74

CHAPTER XV. HAKON THE OLD AT LARGS................................76

CHAPTER XVI. EPILOGUE..77

Early Kings of Norway

Thomas Carlyle

The Icelanders, in their long winter, had a great habit of writing; and were, and still are, excellent in penmanship, says Dahlmann. It is to this fact, that any little history there is of the Norse Kings and their old tragedies, crimes and heroisms, is almost all due. The Icelanders, it seems, not only made beautiful letters on their paper or parchment, but were laudably observant and desirous of accuracy; and have left us such a collection of narratives (Sagas, literally "Says") as, for quantity and quality, is unexampled among rude nations. Snorro Sturleson's History of the Norse Kings is built out of these old Sagas; and has in it a great deal of poetic fire, not a little faithful sagacity applied in sifting and adjusting these old Sagas; and, in a word, deserves, were it once well edited, furnished with accurate maps, chronological summaries, to be reckoned among the great history–books of the world. It is from these sources, greatly aided by accurate, learned and unwearied Dahlmann,[1] the German Professor, that the following rough notes of the early Norway Kings are hastily thrown together. In Histories of England (Rapin's excepted) next to nothing has been shown of the many and strong threads of connection between English affairs and Norse.

CHAPTER I. HARALD HAARFAGR.

Till about the Year of Grace 860 there were no kings in Norway, nothing but numerous jarls,—essentially kinglets, each presiding over a kind of republican or parliamentary little territory; generally striving each to be on some terms of human neighborhood with those about him, but,—in spite of "Fylke Things" (Folk Things, little parish parliaments), and small combinations of these, which had gradually formed themselves,—often reduced to the unhappy state of quarrel with them. Harald Haarfagr was the first to put an end to this state of things, and become memorable and profitable to his country by uniting it under one head and making a kingdom of it; which it has continued to be ever since. His father, Halfdan the Black, had already begun this rough but salutary process,—inspired by the cupidities and instincts, by the faculties and opportunities, which the good genius of this world, beneficent often enough under savage forms, and diligent at all times to diminish anarchy as the world's worst savagery, usually appoints in such cases,—conquest, hard fighting, followed by wise guidance of the conquered;—but it was Harald the Fairhaired, his son, who conspicuously carried it on and completed it. Harald's birth-year, death-year, and chronology in general, are known only by inference and computation; but, by the latest reckoning, he died about the year 933 of our era, a man of eighty-three.

The business of conquest lasted Harald about twelve years (A.D. 860–872?), in which he subdued also the vikings of the out-islands, Orkneys, Shetlands, Hebrides, and Man. Sixty more years were given him to consolidate and regulate what he had conquered, which he did with great judgment, industry and success. His reign altogether is counted to have been of over seventy years.

The beginning of his great adventure was of a romantic character.—youthful love for the beautiful Gyda, a then glorious and famous young lady of those regions, whom the young Harald aspired to marry. Gyda answered his embassy and prayer in a distant, lofty manner: "Her it would not beseem to wed any Jarl or poor creature of that kind; let him do as Gorm of Denmark, Eric of Sweden, Egbert of England, and others had done,—subdue into peace and regulation the confused, contentious bits of jarls round him, and become a king; then, perhaps, she might think of his proposal: till then, not." Harald was struck with this proud answer, which rendered Gyda tenfold more desirable to him. He vowed to let his hair grow, never to cut or even to comb it till this feat were done, and the peerless Gyda his own. He proceeded accordingly to conquer, in fierce battle, a Jarl or two every year, and, at the end of twelve years, had his unkempt (and almost unimaginable) head of hair clipt off,—Jarl Rognwald (Reginald) of More, the most valued and valuable of all his subject-jarls, being promoted to this sublime barber function;—after which King Harald, with head thoroughly cleaned, and hair grown, or growing again to the luxuriant beauty that had no equal in his day, brought home his Gyda, and made her the brightest queen in all the north. He had after her, in succession, or perhaps even simultaneously in some cases, at least six other wives; and by Gyda herself one daughter and four sons.

2

Harald was not to be considered a strict–living man, and he had a great deal of trouble, as we shall see, with the tumultuous ambition of his sons; but he managed his government, aided by Jarl Rognwald and others, in a large, quietly potent, and successful manner; and it lasted in this royal form till his death, after sixty years of it.

These were the times of Norse colonization; proud Norsemen flying into other lands, to freer scenes,—to Iceland, to the Faroe Islands, which were hitherto quite vacant (tenanted only by some mournful hermit, Irish Christian *fakir*, or so); still more copiously to the Orkney and Shetland Isles, the Hebrides and other countries where Norse squatters and settlers already were. Settlement of Iceland, we say; settlement of the Faroe Islands, and, by far the notablest of all, settlement of Normandy by Rolf the Ganger (A.D. 876?).[2]

Rolf, son of Rognwald,[3] was lord of three little islets far north, near the Fjord of Folden, called the Three Vigten Islands; but his chief means of living was that of sea robbery; which, or at least Rolf's conduct in which, Harald did not approve of. In the Court of Harald, sea–robbery was strictly forbidden as between Harald's own countries, but as against foreign countries it continued to be the one profession for a gentleman; thus, I read, Harald's own chief son, King Eric that afterwards was, had been at sea in such employments ever since his twelfth year. Rolf's crime, however, was that in coming home from one of these expeditions, his crew having fallen short of victual, Rolf landed with them on the shore of Norway, and in his strait, drove in some cattle there (a crime by law) and proceeded to kill and eat; which, in a little while, he heard that King Harald was on foot to inquire into and punish; whereupon Rolf the Ganger speedily got into his ships again, got to the coast of France with his sea– robbers, got infeftment by the poor King of France in the fruitful, shaggy desert which is since called Normandy, land of the Northmen; and there, gradually felling the forests, banking the rivers, tilling the fields, became, during the next two centuries, Wilhelmus Conquaestor, the man famous to England, and momentous at this day, not to England alone, but to all speakers of the English tongue, now spread from side to side of the world in a wonderful degree. Tancred of Hauteville and his Italian Normans, though important too, in Italy, are not worth naming in comparison. This is a feracious earth, and the grain of mustard–seed will grow to miraculous extent in some cases.

Harald's chief helper, counsellor, and lieutenant was the above–mentioned Jarl Rognwald of More, who had the honor to cut Harald's dreadful head of hair. This Rognwald was father of Turf–Einar, who first invented peat in the Orkneys, finding the wood all gone

3

there; and is remembered to this day. Einar, being come to these islands by King Harald's permission, to see what he could do in them,—islands inhabited by what miscellany of Picts, Scots, Norse squatters we do not know,—found the indispensable fuel all wasted. Turf–Einar too may be regarded as a benefactor to his kind. He was, it appears, a bastard; and got no coddling from his father, who disliked him, partly perhaps, because "he was ugly and blind of an eye,"—got no flattering even on his conquest of the Orkneys and invention of peat. Here is the parting speech his father made to him on fitting him out with a "long–ship" (ship of war, "dragon–ship," ancient seventy–four), and sending him forth to make a living for himself in the world: "It were best if thou never camest back, for I have small hope that thy people will have honor by thee; thy mother's kin throughout is slavish."

Harald Haarfagr had a good many sons and daughters; the daughters he married mostly to jarls of due merit who were loyal to him; with the sons, as remarked above, he had a great deal of trouble. They were ambitious, stirring fellows, and grudged at their finding so little promotion from a father so kind to his jarls; sea–robbery by no means an adequate career for the sons of a great king, two of them, Halfdan Haaleg (Long–leg), and Gudrod Ljome (Gleam), jealous of the favors won by the great Jarl Rognwald. surrounded him in his house one night, and burnt him and sixty men to death there. That was the end of Rognwald, the invaluable jarl, always true to Haarfagr; and distinguished in world history by producing Rolf the Ganger, author of the Norman Conquest of England, and Turf–Einar, who invented peat in the Orkneys. Whether Rolf had left Norway at this time there is no chronology to tell me. As to Rolf's surname, "Ganger," there are various hypotheses; the likeliest, perhaps, that Rolf was so weighty a man no horse (small Norwegian horses, big ponies rather) could carry him, and that he usually walked, having a mighty stride withal, and great velocity on foot.

One of these murderers of Jarl Rognwald quietly set himself in Rognwald's place, the other making for Orkney to serve Turf–Einar in like fashion. Turf–Einar, taken by surprise, fled to the mainland; but returned, days or perhaps weeks after, ready for battle, fought with Halfdan, put his party to flight, and at next morning's light searched the island and slew all the men he found. As to Halfdan Long–leg himself, in fierce memory of his own murdered father, Turf–Einar "cut an eagle on his back," that is to say, hewed the ribs from each side of the spine and turned them out like the wings of a spread–eagle: a mode of Norse vengeance fashionable at that time in extremely aggravated cases!

Harald Haarfagr, in the mean time, had descended upon the Rognwald scene, not in mild mood towards the new jarl there; indignantly dismissed said jarl, and appointed a brother of Rognwald (brother, notes Dahlmann), though Rognwald had left other sons. Which done, Haarfagr sailed with all speed to the Orkneys, there to avenge that cutting of an eagle on the human back on Turf–Einar's part. Turf–Einar did not resist; submissively met the angry Haarfagr, said he left it all, what had been done, what provocation there had been, to Haarfagr's own equity and greatness of mind. Magnanimous Haarfagr inflicted a fine of sixty marks in gold, which was paid in ready money by Turf–Einar, and so the matter ended.

CHAPTER II. ERIC BLOOD–AXE AND BROTHERS.

In such violent courses Haarfagr's sons, I know not how many of them, had come to an untimely end; only Eric, the accomplished sea–rover, and three others remained to him. Among these four sons, rather impatient for property and authority of their own, King Harald, in his old days, tried to part his kingdom in some eligible and equitable way, and retire from the constant press of business, now becoming burdensome to him. To each of them he gave a kind of kingdom; Eric, his eldest son, to be head king, and the others to be feudatory under him, and pay a certain yearly contribution; an arrangement which did not answer well at all. Head–King Eric insisted on his tribute; quarrels arose as to the payment, considerable fighting and disturbance, bringing fierce destruction from King Eric upon many valiant but too stubborn Norse spirits, and among the rest upon all his three brothers, which got him from the Norse populations the surname of *Blod–axe*, "Eric Blood–axe," his title in history. One of his brothers he had killed in battle before his old father's life ended; this brother was Bjorn, a peaceable, improving, trading economic Under–king, whom the others mockingly called "Bjorn the Chapman." The great–grandson of this Bjorn became extremely distinguished by and by as *Saint* Olaf. Head–King Eric seems to have had a violent wife, too. She was thought to have poisoned one of her other brothers–in–law. Eric Blood–axe had by no means a gentle life of it in this world, trained to sea–robbery on the coasts of England, Scotland, Ireland and France, since his twelfth year.

Old King Fairhair, at the age of seventy, had another son, to whom was given the name of Hakon. His mother was a slave in Fairhair's house; slave by ill–luck of war, though nobly enough born. A strange adventure connects this Hakon with England and King Athelstan, who was then entering upon his great career there. Short while after this Hakon came into the world, there entered Fairhair's palace, one evening as Fairhair sat Feasting, an English ambassador or messenger, bearing in his hand, as gift from King Athelstan, a magnificent sword, with gold hilt and other fine trimmings, to the great Harald, King of Norway. Harald took the sword, drew it, or was half drawing it, admiringly from the scabbard, when the English excellency broke into a scornful laugh, "Ha, ha; thou art now the feudatory of my English king; thou hast accepted the sword from him, and art now his man!" (acceptance of a sword in that manner being the symbol of investiture in those days.) Harald looked a trifle flurried, it is probable; but held in his wrath, and did no damage to the tricksy Englishman. He kept the matter in his mind, however, and next summer little Hakon, having got his weaning done,—one of the prettiest, healthiest little creatures,—Harald sent him off, under charge of "Hauk" (Hawk so called), one of his Principal, warriors, with order, "Take him to England," and instructions what to do with him there. And accordingly, one evening, Hauk, with thirty men escorting, strode into Athelstan's high dwelling (where situated, how built, whether with logs like Harald's, I cannot specifically say), into Athelstan's high presence, and silently set the wild little cherub upon Athelstan's knee. "What is this?" asked Athelstan, looking at the little cherub. "This is King Harald's son, whom a serving–maid bore to him, and whom he now gives thee as foster–child!" Indignant Athelstan drew his sword, as if to do the gift a mischief; but Hauk said, "Thou hast taken him on thy knee [common symbol of adoption]; thou canst kill him if thou wilt; but thou dost not thereby kill all the sons of Harald." Athelstan straightway took milder thoughts; brought up, and carefully educated Hakon; from whom, and this singular adventure, came, before very long, the first tidings of Christianity into Norway.

Harald Haarfagr, latterly withdrawn from all kinds of business, died at the age of eighty–three—about A.D. 933, as is computed; nearly contemporary in death with the first Danish King, Gorm the Old, who had done a corresponding feat in reducing Denmark under one head. Remarkable old men, these two first kings; and possessed of gifts for bringing Chaos a little nearer to the form of Cosmos; possessed, in fact, of loyalties to Cosmos, that is to say, of authentic virtues in the savage state, such as have been needed in all societies at their incipience in this world; a kind of "virtues" hugely in discredit at present, but not unlikely to be needed again, to the astonishment of careless persons, before all is done!

CHAPTER III. HAKON THE GOOD.

Eric Blood–axe, whose practical reign is counted to have begun about A.D. 930, had by this time, or within a year or so of this time, pretty much extinguished all his brother kings, and crushed down recalcitrant spirits, in his violent way; but had naturally become entirely unpopular in Norway, and filled it with silent discontent and even rage against him. Hakon Fairhair's last son, the little foster–child of Athelstan in England, who had been baptized and carefully educated, was come to his fourteenth or fifteenth year at his father's death; a very shining youth, as Athelstan saw with just pleasure. So soon as the few preliminary preparations had been settled, Hakon, furnished with a ship or two by Athelstan, suddenly appeared in Norway got acknowledged by the Peasant Thing in Trondhjem "the news of which flew over Norway, like fire through dried grass," says an old chronicler. So that Eric, with his Queen Gunhild, and seven small children, had to run; no other shift for Eric. They went to the Orkneys first of all, then to England, and he "got Northumberland as earldom," I vaguely hear, from Athelstan. But Eric soon died, and his queen, with her children, went back to the Orkneys in search of refuge or help; to little purpose there or elsewhere. From Orkney she went to Denmark, where Harald Blue–tooth took her poor eldest boy as foster–child; but I fear did not very faithfully keep that promise. The Danes had been robbing extensively during the late tumults in Norway; this the Christian Hakon, now established there, paid in kind, and the two countries were at war; so that Gunhild's little boy was a welcome card in the hand of Blue–tooth.

Hakon proved a brilliant and successful king; regulated many things, public law among others (Gule–Thing Law, *Frost–Thing* Law: these are little codes of his accepted by their respective Things, and had a salutary effect in their time); with prompt dexterity he drove back the Blue–tooth foster–son invasions every time they came; and on the whole gained for himself the name of Hakon the Good. These Danish invasions were a frequent source of trouble to him, but his greatest and continual trouble was that of extirpating heathen idolatry from Norway, and introducing the Christian Evangel in its stead. His transcendent anxiety to achieve this salutary enterprise was all along his grand difficulty and stumbling–block; the heathen opposition to it being also rooted and great. Bishops and priests from England Hakon had, preaching and baptizing what they could, but making only slow progress; much too slow for Hakon's zeal. On the other hand, every Yule–tide, when the chief heathen were assembled in his own palace on their grand

7

sacrificial festival, there was great pressure put upon Hakon, as to sprinkling with horse–blood, drinking Yule–beer, eating horse–flesh, and the other distressing rites; the whole of which Hakon abhorred, and with all his steadfastness strove to reject utterly. Sigurd, Jarl of Lade (Trondhjem), a liberal heathen, not openly a Christian, was ever a wise counsellor and conciliator in such affairs; and proved of great help to Hakon. Once, for example, there having risen at a Yule–feast, loud, almost stormful demand that Hakon, like a true man and brother, should drink Yule–beer with them in their sacred hightide, Sigurd persuaded him to comply, for peace's sake, at least, in form. Hakon took the cup in his left hand (excellent hot *beer*), and with his right cut the sign of the cross above it, then drank a draught. "Yes; but what is this with the king's right hand?" cried the company. "Don't you see?" answered shifty Sigurd; "he makes the sign of Thor's hammer before drinking!" which quenched the matter for the time.

Horse–flesh, horse–broth, and the horse ingredient generally, Hakon all but inexorably declined. By Sigurd's pressing exhortation and entreaty, he did once take a kettle of horsebroth by the handle, with a good deal of linen–quilt or towel interposed, and did open his lips for what of steam could insinuate itself. At another time he consented to a particle of horse–liver, intending privately, I guess, to keep it outside the gullet, and smuggle it away without swallowing; but farther than this not even Sigurd could persuade him to go. At the Things held in regard to this matter Hakon's success was always incomplete; now and then it was plain failure, and Hakon had to draw back till a better time. Here is one specimen of the response he got on such an occasion; curious specimen, withal, of antique parliamentary eloquence from an Anti–Christian Thing.

At a Thing of all the Fylkes of Trondhjem, Thing held at Froste in that region, King Hakon, with all the eloquence he had, signified that it was imperatively necessary that all Bonders and sub–Bonders should become Christians, and believe in one God, Christ the Son of Mary; renouncing entirely blood sacrifices and heathen idols; should keep every seventh day holy, abstain from labor that day, and even from food, devoting the day to fasting and sacred meditation. Whereupon, by way of universal answer, arose a confused universal murmur of entire dissent. "Take away from us our old belief, and also our time for labor!" murmured they in angry astonishment; "how can even the land be got tilled in that way?" "We cannot work if we don't get food," said the hand laborers and slaves. "It lies in King Hakon's blood," remarked others; "his father and all his kindred were apt to be stingy about food, though liberal enough with money." At length, one Osbjorn (or Bear of the Asen or Gods, what we now call Osborne), one Osbjorn of Medalhusin

Gulathal, stept forward, and said, in a distinct manner, "We Bonders (peasant proprietors)thought, King Hakon, when thou heldest thy first Thing–day here in Trondhjem, and we took thee for our king, and received our hereditary lands from thee again that we had got heaven itself. But now we know not how it is, whether we have won freedom, or whether thou intendest anew to make us slaves, with this wonderful proposal that we should renounce our faith, which our fathers before us have held, and all our ancestors as well, first in the age of burial by burning, and now in that of earth burial; and yet these departed ones were much our superiors, and their faith, too, has brought prosperity to us. Thee, at the same time, we have loved so much that we raised thee to manage all the laws of the land, and speak as their voice to us all. And even now it is our will and the vote of all Bonders to keep that paction which thou gavest us here on the Thing at Froste, and to maintain thee as king so long as any of us Bonders who are here upon the Thing has life left, provided thou, king, wilt go fairly to work, and demand of us only such things as are not impossible. But if thou wilt fix upon this thing with so great obstinacy, and employ force and power, in that case, we Bonders have taken the resolution, all of us, to fall away from thee, and to take for ourselves another head, who will so behave that we may enjoy in freedom the belief which is agreeable to us. Now shalt thou, king, choose one of these two courses before the Thing disperse." "Whereupon," adds the Chronicle, "all the Bonders raised a mighty shout, 'Yes, we will have it so, as has been said.'" So that Jarl Sigurd had to intervene, and King Hakon to choose for the moment the milder branch of the alternative.[4] At other Things Hakon was more or less successful. All his days, by such methods as there were, he kept pressing forward with this great enterprise; and on the whole did thoroughly shake asunder the old edifice of heathendom, and fairly introduce some foundation for the new and better rule of faith and life among his people. Sigurd, Jarl of Lade, his wise counsellor in all these matters, is also a man worthy of notice.

Hakon's arrangements against the continual invasions of Eric's sons, with Danish Blue–tooth backing them, were manifold, and for a long time successful. He appointed, after consultation and consent in the various Things, so many war–ships, fully manned and ready, to be furnished instantly on the King's demand by each province or fjord; watch–fires, on fit places, from hill to hill all along the coast, were to be carefully set up, carefully maintained in readiness, and kindled on any alarm of war. By such methods Blue–tooth and Co.'s invasions were for a long while triumphantly, and even rapidly, one and all of them, beaten back, till at length they seemed as if intending to cease altogether, and leave Hakon alone of them. But such was not their issue after all. The sons of Eric

9

had only abated under constant discouragement, had not finally left off from what seemed their one great feasibility in life. Gunhild, their mother, was still with them: a most contriving, fierce–minded, irreconcilable woman, diligent and urgent on them, in season and out of season; and as for King Blue–tooth, he was at all times ready to help, with his good–will at least.

That of the alarm–fires on Hakon's part was found troublesome by his people; sometimes it was even hurtful and provoking (lighting your alarm–fires and rousing the whole coast and population, when it was nothing but some paltry viking with a couple of ships); in short, the alarm–signal system fell into disuse, and good King Hakon himself, in the first place, paid the penalty. It is counted, by the latest commentators, to have been about A.D. 961, sixteenth or seventeenth year of Hakon's pious, valiant, and worthy reign. Being at a feast one day, with many guests, on the Island of Stord, sudden announcement came to him that ships from the south were approaching in quantity, and evidently ships of war. This was the biggest of all the Blue–tooth foster–son invasions; and it was fatal to Hakon the Good that night. Eyvind the Skaldaspillir (annihilator of all other Skalds), in his famed *Hakon's Song*, gives account, and, still more pertinently, the always practical Snorro. Danes in great multitude, six to one, as people afterwards computed, springing swiftly to land, and ranking themselves; Hakon, nevertheless, at once deciding not to take to his ships and run, but to fight there, one to six; fighting, accordingly, in his most splendid manner, and at last gloriously prevailing; routing and scattering back to their ships and flight homeward these six–to–one Danes. "During the struggle of the fight," says Snorro, "he was very conspicuous among other men; and while the sun shone, his bright gilded helmet glanced, and thereby many weapons were directed at him. One of his henchmen, Eyvind Finnson (i.e. Skaldaspillir, the poet), took a hat, and put it over the king's helmet. Now, among the hostile first leaders were two uncles of the Ericsons, brothers of Gunhild, great champions both; Skreya, the elder of them, on the disappearance of the glittering helmet, shouted boastfully, 'Does the king of the Norsemen hide himself, then, or has he fled? Where now is the golden helmet?' And so saying, Skreya, and his brother Alf with him, pushed on like fools or madmen. The king said, 'Come on in that way, and you shall find the king of the Norsemen.'" And in a short space of time braggart Skreya did come up, swinging his sword, and made a cut at the king; but Thoralf the Strong, an Icelander, who fought at the king's side, dashed his shield so hard against Skreya, that he tottered with the shock. On the same instant the king takes his sword "quernbiter" (able to cut *querns* or millstones) with both hands, and hews Skreya through helm and head, cleaving him down to the shoulders. Thoralf also slew

10

Alf. That was what they got by such over–hasty search for the king of the Norsemen.[5]

Snorro considers the fall of these two champion uncles as the crisis of the fight; the Danish force being much disheartened by such a sight, and King Hakon now pressing on so hard that all men gave way before him, the battle on the Ericson part became a whirl of recoil; and in a few minutes more a torrent of mere flight and haste to get on board their ships, and put to sea again; in which operation many of them were drowned, says Snorro; survivors making instant sail for Denmark in that sad condition.

This seems to have been King Hakon's finest battle, and the most conspicuous of his victories, due not a little to his own grand qualities shown on the occasion. But, alas! it was his last also. He was still zealously directing the chase of that mad Danish flight, or whirl of recoil towards their ships, when an arrow, shot Most likely at a venture, hit him under the left armpit; and this proved his death.

He was helped into his ship, and made sail for Alrekstad, where his chief residence in those parts was; but had to stop at a smaller place of his (which had been his mother's, and where he himself was born)—a place called Hella (the Flat Rock), still known as "Hakon's Hella," faint from loss of blood, and crushed down as he had never before felt. Having no son and only one daughter, he appointed these invasive sons of Eric to be sent for, and if he died to become king; but to "spare his friends and kindred." "If a longer life be granted me," he said, "I will go out of this land to Christian men, and do penance for what I have committed against God. But if I die in the country of the heathen, let me have such burial as you yourselves think fittest." These are his last recorded words. And in heathen fashion he was buried, and besung by Eyvind and the Skalds, though himself a zealously Christian king. Hakon the *Good*; so one still finds him worthy of being called. The sorrow on Hakon's death, Snorro tells us, was so great and universal, "that he was lamented both by friends and enemies; and they said that never again would Norway see such a king."

CHAPTER IV. HARALD GREYFELL AND BROTHERS.

Eric's sons, four or five of them, with a Harald at the top, now at once got Norway in hand, all of it but Trondhjem, as king and under–kings; and made a severe time of it for those who had been, or seemed to be, their enemies. Excellent Jarl Sigurd, always so useful to Hakon and his country, was killed by them; and they came to repent that before very long. The slain Sigurd left a son, Hakon, as Jarl, who became famous in the northern world by and by. This Hakon, and him only, would the Trondhjemers accept as sovereign. "Death to him, then," said the sons of Eric, but only in secret, till they had got their hands free and were ready; which was not yet for some years. Nay, Hakon, when actually attacked, made good resistance, and threatened to cause trouble. Nor did he by any means get his death from these sons of Eric at this time, or till long afterwards at all, from one of their kin, as it chanced. On the contrary, he fled to Denmark now, and by and by managed to come back, to their cost.

Among their other chief victims were two cousins of their own, Tryggve and Gudrod, who had been honest under–kings to the late head–king, Hakon the Good; but were now become suspect, and had to fight for their lives, and lose them in a tragic manner. Tryggve had a son, whom we shall hear of. Gudrod, son of worthy Bjorn the Chapman, was grandfather of Saint Olaf, whom all men have heard of,—who has a church in Southwark even, and another in Old Jewry, to this hour. In all these violences, Gunhild, widow of the late king Eric, was understood to have a principal hand. She had come back to Norway with her sons; and naturally passed for the secret adviser and Maternal President in whatever of violence went on; always reckoned a fell, vehement, relentless personage where her own interests were concerned. Probably as things settled, her influence on affairs grew less. At least one hopes so; and, in the Sagas, hears less and less of her, and before long nothing.

Harald, the head–king in this Eric fraternity, does not seem to have been a bad man,—the contrary indeed; but his position was untowardly, full of difficulty and contradictions. Whatever Harald could accomplish for behoof of Christianity, or real benefit to Norway, in these cross circumstances, he seems to have done in a modest and honest manner. He got the name of *Greyfell* from his people on a very trivial account, but seemingly with perfect good humor on their part. Some Iceland trader had brought a cargo of furs to Trondhjem (Lade) for sale; sale being slacker than the Icelander wished, he presented a chosen specimen, cloak, doublet, or whatever it was, to Harald; who wore it with acceptance in public, and rapidly brought disposal of the Icelander's stock, and the surname of *Greyfell* to himself. His under–kings and he were certainly not popular, though I almost think Greyfell himself, in absence of his mother and the under–kings, might have been so. But here they all were, and had wrought great trouble in Norway. "Too many of them," said everybody; "too many of these courts and court people, eating

12

up any substance that there is." For the seasons withal, two or three of them in succession, were bad for grass, much more for grain; no *herring* came either; very cleanness of teeth was like to come in Eyvind Skaldaspillir's opinion. This scarcity became at last their share of the great Famine Of A.D. 975, which desolated Western Europe (see the poem in the Saxon Chronicle). And all this by Eyvind Skaldaspillir, and the heathen Norse in general, was ascribed to anger of the heathen gods. Discontent in Norway, and especially in Eyvind Skaldaspillir, seems to have been very great.

Whereupon exile Hakon, Jarl Sigurd's son, bestirs himself in Denmark, backed by old King Blue–tooth, and begins invading and encroaching in a miscellaneous way; especially intriguing and contriving plots all round him. An unfathomably cunning kind of fellow, as well as an audacious and strong–handed! Intriguing in Trondhjem, where he gets the under–king, Greyfell's brother, fallen upon and murdered; intriguing with Gold Harald, a distinguished cousin or nephew of King Blue–tooth's, who had done fine viking work, and gained, such wealth that he got the epithet of "Gold," and who now was infinitely desirous of a share in Blue–tooth's kingdom as the proper finish to these sea–rovings. He even ventured one day to make publicly a distinct proposal that way to King Harald Blue–tooth himself; who flew into thunder and lightning at the mere mention of it; so that none durst speak to him for several days afterwards. Of both these Haralds Hakon was confidential friend; and needed all his skill to walk without immediate annihilation between such a pair of dragons, and work out Norway for himself withal. In the end he found he must take solidly to Blue–tooth's side of the question; and that they two must provide a recipe for Gold Harald and Norway both at once.

"It is as much as your life is worth to speak again of sharing this Danish kingdom," said Hakon very privately to Gold Harald; "but could not you, my golden friend, be content with Norway for a kingdom, if one helped you to it?"

"That could I well," answered Harald.

"Then keep me those nine war–ships you have just been rigging for a new viking cruise; have these in readiness when I lift my finger!"

That was the recipe contrived for Gold Harald; recipe for King Greyfell goes into the same vial, and is also ready.

Hitherto the Hakon–Blue–tooth disturbances in Norway had amounted to but little. King Greyfell, a very active and valiant man, has constantly, without much difficulty, repelled these sporadic bits of troubles; but Greyfell, all the same, would willingly have peace with dangerous old Blue–tooth (ever anxious to get his clutches over Norway on any terms) if peace with him could be had. Blue–tooth, too, professes every willingness; inveigles Greyfell, he and Hakon do; to have a friendly meeting on the Danish borders, and not only settle all these quarrels, but generously settle Greyfell in certain fiefs which he claimed in Denmark itself; and so swear everlasting friendship. Greyfell joyfully complies, punctually appears at the appointed day in Lymfjord Sound, the appointed place. Whereupon Hakon gives signal to Gold Harald, "To Lymfjord with these nine ships of yours, swift!" Gold Harald flies to Lymfjord with his ships, challenges King Harald Greyfell to land and fight; which the undaunted Greyfell, though so far outnumbered, does; and, fighting his very best, perishes there, he and almost all his people. Which done, Jarl Hakon, who is in readiness, attacks Gold Harald, the victorious but the wearied; easily beats Gold Harald, takes him prisoner, and instantly hangs and ends him, to the huge joy of King Blue–tooth and Hakon; who now make instant voyage to Norway; drive all the brother under–kings into rapid flight to the Orkneys, to any readiest shelter; and so, under the patronage of Blue–tooth, Hakon, with the title of Jarl, becomes ruler of Norway. This foul treachery done on the brave and honest Harald Greyfell is by some dated about A.D. 969, by Munch, 965, by others, computing out of Snorro only, A.D. 975. For there is always an uncertainty in these Icelandic dates (say rather, rare and rude attempts at dating, without even an "A.D." or other fixed "year one" to go upon in Iceland), though seldom, I think, so large a discrepancy as here.

CHAPTER V. HAKON JARL.

Hakon Jarl, such the style he took, had engaged to pay some kind of tribute to King Blue–tooth, "if he could;" but he never did pay any, pleading always the necessity of his own affairs; with which excuse, joined to Hakon's readiness in things less important, King Blue–tooth managed to content himself, Hakon being always his good neighbor, at least, and the two mutually dependent. In Norway, Hakon, without the title of king, did in a strong–handed, steadfast, and at length, successful way, the office of one; governed Norway (some count) for above twenty years; and, both at home and abroad, had much consideration through most of that time; specially amongst the heathen orthodox, for Hakon Jarl himself was a zealous heathen, fixed in his mind against these chimerical

Christian innovations and unsalutary changes of creed, and would have gladly trampled out all traces of what the last two kings (for Greyfell, also, was an English Christian after his sort) had done in this respect. But he wisely discerned that it was not possible, and that, for peace's sake, he must not even attempt it, but must strike preferably into "perfect toleration," and that of "every one getting to heaven or even to the other goal in his own way." He himself, it is well known, repaired many heathen temples (a great "church builder" in his way!), manufactured many splendid idols, with much gilding and such artistic ornament as there was,—in particular, one huge image of Thor, not forgetting the hammer and appendages, and such a collar (supposed of solid gold, which it was not quite, as we shall hear in time) round the neck of him as was never seen in all the North. How he did his own Yule festivals, with what magnificent solemnity, the horse–eatings, blood–sprinklings, and other sacred rites, need not be told. Something of a "Ritualist," one may perceive; perhaps had Scandinavian Puseyisms in him, and other desperate heathen notions. He was universally believed to have gone into magic, for one thing, and to have dangerous potencies derived from the Devil himself. The dark heathen mind of him struggling vehemently in that strange element, not altogether so unlike our own in some points.

For the rest, he was evidently, in practical matters, a man of sharp, clear insight, of steadfast resolution, diligence, promptitude; and managed his secular matters uncommonly well. Had sixteen Jarls under him, though himself only Hakon Jarl by title; and got obedience from them stricter than any king since Haarfagr had done. Add to which that the country had years excellent for grass and crop, and that the herrings came in exuberance; tokens, to the thinking mind, that Hakon Jarl was a favorite of Heaven.

His fight with the far–famed Jomsvikings was his grandest exploit in public rumor. Jomsburg, a locality not now known, except that it was near the mouth of the River Oder, denoted in those ages the impregnable castle of a certain hotly corporate, or "Sea Robbery Association (limited)," which, for some generations, held the Baltic in terror, and plundered far beyond the Belt,—in the ocean itself, in Flanders and the opulent trading havens there,—above all, in opulent anarchic England, which, for forty years from about this time, was the pirates' Goshen; and yielded, regularly every summer, slaves, Danegelt, and miscellaneous plunder, like no other country Jomsburg or the viking–world had ever known. Palnatoke, Bue, and the other quasi–heroic heads of this establishment are still remembered in the northern parts. *Palnatoke* is the title of a tragedy by Oehlenschlager, which had its run of immortality in Copenhagen some sixty

15

or seventy years ago.

I judge the institution to have been in its floweriest state, probably now in Hakon Jarl's time. Hakon Jarl and these pirates, robbing Hakon's subjects and merchants that frequented him, were naturally in quarrel; and frequent fightings had fallen out, not generally to the profit of the Jomsburgers, who at last determined on revenge, and the rooting out of this obstructive Hakon Jarl. They assembled in force at the Cape of Stad,—in the Firda Fylke; and the fight was dreadful in the extreme, noise of it filling all the north for long afterwards. Hakon, fighting like a lion, could scarcely hold his own,—Death or Victory, the word on both sides; when suddenly, the heavens grew black, and there broke out a terrific storm of thunder and hail, appalling to the human mind,—universe swallowed wholly in black night; only the momentary forked−blazes, the thunder−pealing as of Ragnarok, and the battering hail−torrents, hailstones about the size of an egg. Thor with his hammer evidently acting; but in behalf of whom? The Jomsburgers in the hideous darkness, broken only by flashing thunder−bolts, had a dismal apprehension that it was probably not on their behalf (Thor having a sense of justice in him); and before the storm ended, thirty−five of their seventy ships sheered away, leaving gallant Bue, with the other thirty−five, to follow as they liked, who reproachfully hailed these fugitives, and continued the now hopeless battle. Bue's nose and lips were smashed or cut away; Bue managed, half−articulately, to exclaim, "Ha! the maids ('mays') of Funen will never kiss me more. Overboard, all ye Bue's men!" And taking his two sea−chests, with all the gold he had gained in such life−struggle from of old, sprang overboard accordingly, and finished the affair. Hakon Jarl's renown rose naturally to the transcendent pitch after this exploit. His people, I suppose chiefly the Christian part of them, whispered one to another, with a shudder, "That in the blackest of the thunder−storm, he had taken his youngest little boy, and made away with him; sacrificed him to Thor or some devil, and gained his victory by art−magic, or something worse." Jarl Eric, Hakon's eldest son, without suspicion of art−magic, but already a distinguished viking, became thrice distinguished by his style of sea−fighting in this battle; and awakened great expectations in the viking public; of him we shall hear again.

The Jomsburgers, one might fancy, after this sad clap went visibly down in the world; but the fact is not altogether so. Old King Blue−tooth was now dead, died of a wound got in battle with his unnatural (so−called "natural") son and successor, Otto Svein of the Forked Beard, afterwards king and conqueror of England for a little while; and seldom, perhaps never, had vikingism been in such flower as now. This man's name is Sven in

Swedish, Svend in German, and means boy or lad,—the English "swain." It was at old "Father Bluetooth's funeral—ale" (drunken burial—feast), that Svein, carousing with his Jomsburg chiefs and other choice spirits, generally of the robber class, all risen into height of highest robber enthusiasm, pledged the vow to one another; Svein that he would conquer England (which, in a sense, he, after long struggling, did); and the Jomsburgers that they would ruin and root out Hakon Jarl (which, as we have just seen, they could by no means do), and other guests other foolish things which proved equally unfeasible. Sea—robber volunteers so especially abounding in that time, one perceives how easily the Jomsburgers could recruit themselves, build or refit new robber fleets, man them with the pick of crews, and steer for opulent, fruitful England; where, under Ethelred the Unready, was such a field for profitable enterprise as the viking public never had before or since.

An idle question sometimes rises on me,—idle enough, for it never can be answered in the affirmative or the negative, Whether it was not these same refitted Jomsburgers who appeared some while after this at Red Head Point, on the shore of Angus, and sustained a new severe beating, in what the Scotch still faintly remember as their "Battle of Loncarty"? Beyond doubt a powerful Norse—pirate armament dropt anchor at the Red Head, to the alarm of peaceable mortals, about that time. It was thought and hoped to be on its way for England, but it visibly hung on for several days, deliberating (as was thought) whether they would do this poorer coast the honor to land on it before going farther. Did land, and vigorously plunder and burn south—westward as far as Perth; laid siege to Perth; but brought out King Kenneth on them, and produced that "Battle of Loncarty" which still dwells in vague memory among the Scots. Perhaps it might be the Jomsburgers; perhaps also not; for there were many pirate associations, lasting not from century to century like the Jomsburgers, but only for very limited periods, or from year to year; indeed, it was mainly by such that the splendid thief—harvest of England was reaped in this disastrous time. No Scottish chronicler gives the least of exact date to their famed victory of Loncarty, only that it was achieved by Kenneth III., which will mean some time between A.D. 975 and 994; and, by the order they put it in, probably soon after A.D. 975, or the beginning of this Kenneth's reign. Buchanan's narrative, carefully distilled from all the ancient Scottish sources, is of admirable quality for style and otherwise quiet, brief, with perfect clearness, perfect credibility even, except that semi—miraculous appendage of the Ploughmen, Hay and Sons, always hanging to the tail of it; the grain of possible truth in which can now never be extracted by man's art![6] In brief, what we know is, fragments of ancient human bones and armor have occasionally been ploughed up in this locality, proof positive of ancient fighting here; and the fight fell out not long after Hakon's beating of the Jomsburgers at the Cape of Stad. And in such dim glimmer of wavering twilight, the question whether these of Loncarty were refitted Jomsburgers or not, must be left hanging. Loncarty is now the biggest bleach–field in Queen Victoria's dominions; no village or hamlet there, only the huge bleaching–house and a beautiful field, some six or seven miles northwest of Perth, bordered by the beautiful Tay river on the one side, and by its beautiful tributary Almond on the other; a Loncarty fitted either for bleaching linen, or for a bit of fair duel between nations, in those simple times.

Whether our refitted Jomsburgers had the least thing to do with it is only matter of fancy, but if it were they who here again got a good beating, fancy would be glad to find herself fact. The old piratical kings of Denmark had been at the founding of Jomsburg, and to Svein of the Forked Beard it was still vitally important, but not so to the great Knut, or any king that followed; all of whom had better business than mere thieving; and it was Magnus the Good, of Norway, a man of still higher anti–anarchic qualities, that annihilated it, about a century later.

Hakon Jarl, his chief labors in the world being over, is said to have become very dissolute in his elder days, especially in the matter of women; the wretched old fool, led away by idleness and fulness of bread, which to all of us are well said to be the parents of mischief. Having absolute power, he got into the habit of openly plundering men's pretty daughters and wives from them, and, after a few weeks, sending them back; greatly to the rage of the fierce Norse heart, had there been any means of resisting or revenging. It did, after a little while, prove the ruin and destruction of Hakon the Rich, as he was then called. It opened the door, namely, for entry of Olaf Tryggveson upon the scene,—a very much grander man; in regard to whom the wiles and traps of Hakon proved to be a recipe, not on Tryggveson, but on the wily Hakon himself, as shall now be seen straightway.

CHAPTER VI. OLAF TRYGGVESON.

Hakon, in late times, had heard of a famous stirring person, victorious in various lands and seas, latterly united in sea–robbery with Svein, Prince Royal of Denmark, afterwards King Svein of the Double–beard ("Zvae Skiaeg", *Twa Shag*) or fork–beard, both of whom had already done transcendent feats in the viking way during this copartnery. The fame of Svein, and this stirring personage, whose name was "Ole," and, recently, their stupendous feats in plunder of England, siege of London, and other wonders and splendors of viking glory and success, had gone over all the North, awakening the attention of Hakon and everybody there. The name of "Ole" was enigmatic, mysterious, and even dangerous–looking to Hakon Jarl; who at length sent out a confidential spy to investigate this "Ole;" a feat which the confidential spy did completely accomplish,—by no means to Hakon's profit! The mysterious "Ole" proved to be no other than Olaf, son of Tryggve, destined to blow Hakon Jarl suddenly into destruction, and become famous among the heroes of the Norse world.

Of Olaf Tryggveson one always hopes there might, one day, some real outline of a biography be written; fished from the abysses where (as usual) it welters deep in foul neighborhood for the present. Farther on we intend a few words more upon the matter. But in this place all that concerns us in it limits itself to the two following facts first, that Hakon's confidential spy "found Ole in Dublin;" picked acquaintance with him, got him to confess that he was actually Olaf, son of Tryggve (the Tryggve, whom Blood–axe's fierce widow and her sons had murdered); got him gradually to own that perhaps an expedition into Norway might have its chances; and finally that, under such a wise and loyal guidance as his (the confidential spy's, whose friendship for Tryggveson was so indubitable), he (Tryggveson) would actually try it upon Hakon Jarl, the dissolute old scoundrel. Fact second is, that about the time they two set sail from Dublin on their Norway expedition, Hakon Jarl removed to Trondhjem, then called Lade; intending to pass some months there.

Now just about the time when Tryggveson, spy, and party had landed in Norway, and were advancing upon Lade, with what support from the public could be got, dissolute old Hakon Jarl had heard of one Gudrun, a Bonder's wife, unparalleled in beauty, who was called in those parts, "Sunbeam of the Grove" (so inexpressibly lovely); and sent off a couple of thralls to bring her to him. "Never," answered Gudrun; "never," her indignant husband; in a tone dangerous and displeasing to these Court thralls; who had to leave rapidly, but threatened to return in better strength before long. Whereupon, instantly, the indignant Bonder and his Sunbeam of the Grove sent out their war–arrow, rousing all the country into angry promptitude, and more than one perhaps into greedy hope of revenge for their own injuries. The rest of Hakon's history now rushes on with extreme rapidity.

Sunbeam of the Grove, when next demanded of her Bonder, has the whole neighborhood assembled in arms round her; rumor of Tryggveson is fast making it the whole country. Hakon's insolent messengers are cut in pieces; Hakon finds he cannot fly under cover too soon. With a single slave he flies that same night;—but whitherward? Can think of no safe place, except to some old mistress of his, who lives retired in that neighborhood, and has some pity or regard for the wicked old Hakon. Old mistress does receive him, pities him, will do all she can to protect and hide him. But how, by what uttermost stretch of female artifice hide him here; every one will search here first of all! Old mistress, by the slave's help, extemporizes a cellar under the floor of her pig-house; sticks Hakon and slave into that, as the one safe seclusion she can contrive. Hakon and slave, begrunted by the pigs above them, tortured by the devils within and about them, passed two days in circumstances more and more horrible. For they heard, through their light-slit and breathing-slit, the triumph of Tryggveson proclaiming itself by Tryggveson's own lips, who had mounted a big boulder near by and was victoriously speaking to the people, winding up with a promise of honors and rewards to whoever should bring him wicked old Hakon's head. Wretched Hakon, justly suspecting his slave, tried to at least keep himself awake. Slave did keep himself awake till Hakon dozed or slept, then swiftly cut off Hakon's head, and plunged out with it to the presence of Tryggveson. Tryggveson, detesting the traitor, useful as the treachery was, cut off the slave's head too, had it hung up along with Hakon's on the pinnacle of the Lade Gallows, where the populace pelted both heads with stones and many curses, especially the more important of the two. "Hakon the Bad" ever henceforth, instead of Hakon the Rich.

This was the end of Hakon Jarl, the last support of heathenry in Norway, among other characteristics he had: a stronghanded, hard-headed, very relentless, greedy and wicked being. He is reckoned to have ruled in Norway, or mainly ruled, either in the struggling or triumphant state, for about thirty years (965–995?). He and his seemed to have formed, by chance rather than design, the chief opposition which the Haarfagr posterity throughout its whole course experienced in Norway. Such the cost to them of killing good Jarl Sigurd, in Greyfell's time! For "curses, like chickens," do sometimes visibly "come home to feed," as they always, either visibly or else invisibly, are punctually sure to do.

Hakon Jarl is considerably connected with the *Faroer Saga* often mentioned there, and comes out perfectly in character; an altogether worldly-wise man of the roughest type, not without a turn for practicality of kindness to those who would really be of use to him. His tendencies to magic also are not forgotten.

Hakon left two sons, Eric and Svein, often also mentioned in this Saga. On their father's death they fled to Sweden, to Denmark, and were busy stirring up troubles in those countries against Olaf Tryggveson; till at length, by a favorable combination, under their auspices chiefly, they got his brief and noble reign put an end to. Nay, furthermore, Jarl Eric left sons, especially an elder son, named also Eric, who proved a sore affliction, and a continual stone of stumbling to a new generation of Haarfagrs, and so continued the curse of Sigurd's murder upon them.

Towards the end of this Hakon's reign it was that the discovery of America took place (985). Actual discovery, it appears, by Eric the Red, an Icelander; concerning which there has been abundant investigation and discussion in our time. *Ginnungagap* (Roaring Abyss) is thought to be the mouth of Behring's Straits in Baffin's Bay; *Big Helloland*, the coast from Cape Walsingham to near Newfoundland; *Little Helloland*, Newfoundland itself. *Markland* was Lower Canada, New Brunswick, and Nova Scotia. Southward thence to Chesapeake Bay was called *Wine Land* (wild grapes still grow in Rhode Island, and more luxuriantly further south). *White Man's Land*, called also *Great Ireland*, is supposed to mean the two Carolinas, down to the Southern Cape of Florida. In Dahlmann's opinion, the Irish themselves might even pretend to have probably been the first discoverers of America; they had evidently got to Iceland itself before the Norse exiles found it out. It appears to be certain that, from the end of the tenth century to the early part of the fourteenth, there was a dim knowledge of those distant shores extant in the Norse mind, and even some straggling series of visits thither by roving Norsemen; though, as only danger, difficulty, and no profit resulted, the visits ceased, and the whole matter sank into oblivion, and, but for the Icelandic talent of writing in the long winter nights, would never have been heard of by posterity at all.

CHAPTER VII. REIGN OF OLAF TRYGGVESON.

Olaf Tryggveson (A.D. 995–1000) also makes a great figure in the Faroer Saga, and recounts there his early troubles, which were strange and many. He is still reckoned a grand hero of the North, though his *vates* now is only Snorro Sturleson of Iceland. Tryggveson had indeed many adventures in the world. His poor mother, Astrid, was obliged to fly, on murder of her husband by Gunhild,—to fly for life, three months before he, her little Olaf, was born. She lay concealed in reedy islands, fled through trackless forests; reached her father's with the little baby in her arms, and lay deep–hidden there, tended only by her father himself; Gunhild's pursuit being so incessant, and keen as with sleuth-hounds. Poor Astrid had to fly again, deviously to Sweden, to Esthland (Esthonia), to Russia. In Esthland she was sold as a slave, quite parted from her boy,—who also was sold, and again sold; but did at last fall in with a kinsman high in the Russian service; did from him find redemption and help, and so rose, in a distinguished manner, to manhood, victorious self-help, and recovery of his kingdom at last. He even met his mother again, he as king of Norway, she as one wonderfully lifted out of darkness into new life and happiness still in store.

Grown to manhood, Tryggveson,—now become acquainted with his birth, and with his, alas, hopeless claims,—left Russia for the one profession open to him, that of sea-robbery; and did feats without number in that questionable line in many seas and scenes,—in England latterly, and most conspicuously of all. In one of his courses thither, after long labors in the Hebrides, Man, Wales, and down the western shores to the very Land's End and farther, he paused at the Scilly Islands for a little while. He was told of a wonderful Christian hermit living strangely in these sea-solitudes; had the curiosity to seek him out, examine, question, and discourse with him; and, after some reflection, accepted Christian baptism from the venerable man. In Snorro the story is involved in miracle, rumor, and fable; but the fact itself seems certain, and is very interesting; the great, wild, noble soul of fierce Olaf opening to this wonderful gospel of tidings from beyond the world, tidings which infinitely transcended all else he had ever heard or dreamt of! It seems certain he was baptized here; date not fixable; shortly before poor heart-broken Dunstan's death, or shortly after; most English churches, monasteries especially, lying burnt, under continual visitation of the Danes. Olaf such baptism notwithstanding, did not quit his viking profession; indeed, what other was there for him in the world as yet?

We mentioned his occasional copartneries with Svein of the Double-beard, now become King of Denmark, but the greatest of these, and the alone interesting at this time, is their joint invasion of England, and Tryggveson's exploits and fortunes there some years after that adventure of baptism in the Scilly Isles. Svein and he "were above a year in England together," this time: they steered up the Thames with three hundred ships and many fighters; siege, or at least furious assault, of London was their first or main enterprise, but it did not succeed. The Saxon Chronicle gives date to it, A.D. 994, and names expressly, as Svein's co-partner, "Olaus, king of Norway,"—which he was as yet far from being; but in regard to the Year of Grace the Saxon Chronicle is to be held indisputable, and, indeed, has the field to itself in this matter. Famed Olaf Tryggveson, seen visibly at the siege of London, year 994, it throws a kind of momentary light to us over that disastrous whirlpool of miseries and confusions, all dark and painful to the fancy otherwise! This big voyage and furious siege of London is Svein Double–beard's first real attempt to fulfil that vow of his at Father Blue–tooth's "funeral ale," and conquer England,—which it is a pity he could not yet do. Had London now fallen to him, it is pretty evident all England must have followed, and poor England, with Svein as king over it, been delivered from immeasurable woes, which had to last some two–and–twenty years farther, before this result could be arrived at. But finding London impregnable for the moment (no ship able to get athwart the bridge, and many Danes perishing in the attempt to do it by swimming), Svein and Olaf turned to other enterprises; all England in a manner lying open to them, turn which way they liked. They burnt and plundered over Kent, over Hampshire, Sussex; they stormed far and wide; world lying all before them where to choose. Wretched Ethelred, as the one invention he could fall upon, offered them Danegelt (16,000 pounds of silver this year, but it rose in other years as high as 48,000 pounds); the desperate Ethelred, a clear method of quenching fire by pouring oil on it! Svein and Olaf accepted; withdrew to Southampton,—Olaf at least did,—till the money was got ready. Strange to think of, fierce Svein of the Double–beard, and conquest of England by him; this had at last become the one salutary result which remained for that distracted, down–trodden, now utterly chaotic and anarchic country. A conquering Svein, followed by an ably and earnestly administrative, as well as conquering, Knut (whom Dahlmann compares to Charlemagne), were thus by the mysterious destinies appointed the effective saviors of England.

Tryggveson, on this occasion, was a good while at Southampton; and roamed extensively about, easily victorious over everything, if resistance were attempted, but finding little or none; and acting now in a peaceable or even friendly capacity. In the Southampton country he came in contact with the then Bishop of Winchester, afterwards Archbishop of Canterbury, excellent Elphegus, still dimly decipherable to us as a man of great natural discernment, piety, and inborn veracity; a hero–soul, probably of real brotherhood with Olaf's own. He even made court visits to King Ethelred; one visit to him at Andover of a very serious nature. By Elphegus, as we can discover, he was introduced into the real depths of the Christian faith. Elphegus, with due solemnity of apparatus, in presence of the king, at Andover, baptized Olaf anew, and to him Olaf engaged that he would never plunder in England any more; which promise, too, he kept. In fact, not long after, Svein's conquest of England being in an evidently forward state, Tryggveson (having made, withal, a great English or Irish marriage,—a dowager Princess, who had voluntarily fallen in love with him,—see Snorro for this fine romantic fact!) mainly resided in our island for two or three years, or else in Dublin, in the precincts of the Danish Court there in the Sister Isle. Accordingly it was in Dublin, as above noted, that Hakon's spy found him; and from the Liffey that his squadron sailed, through the Hebrides, through the Orkneys, plundering and baptizing in their strange way, towards such success as we have seen.

Tryggveson made a stout, and, in effect, victorious and glorious struggle for himself as king. Daily and hourly vigilant to do so, often enough by soft and even merry methods, for he was a witty, jocund man, and had a fine ringing laugh in him, and clear pregnant words ever ready,—or if soft methods would not serve, then by hard and even hardest he put down a great deal of miscellaneous anarchy in Norway; was especially busy against heathenism (devil–worship and its rites): this, indeed, may be called the focus and heart of all his royal endeavor in Norway, and of all the troubles he now had with his people there. For this was a serious, vital, all–comprehending matter; devil–worship, a thing not to be tolerated one moment longer than you could by any method help! Olaf's success was intermittent, of varying complexion; but his effort, swift or slow, was strong and continual; and on the whole he did succeed. Take a sample or two of that wonderful conversion process:—

At one of his first Things he found the Bonders all assembled in arms; resolute to the death seemingly, against his proposal and him. Tryggveson said little; waited impassive, "What your reasons are, good men?" One zealous Bonder started up in passionate parliamentary eloquence; but after a sentence or two, broke down; one, and then another, and still another, and remained all three staring in open–mouthed silence there! The peasant–proprietors accepted the phenomenon as ludicrous, perhaps partly as miraculous withal, and consented to baptism this time.

On another occasion of a Thing, which had assembled near some heathen temple to meet him,—temple where Hakon Jarl had done much repairing, and set up many idol figures and sumptuous ornaments, regardless of expense, especially a very big and splendid Thor, with massive gold collar round the neck of him, not the like of it in Norway,—King Olaf Tryggveson was clamorously invited by the Bonders to step in there, enlighten his eyes, and partake of the sacred rites. Instead of which he rushed into the temple with his armed men; smashed down, with his own battle–axe, the god Thor, prostrate on the ground at one stroke, to set an example; and, in a few minutes, had the whole Hakon Pantheon wrecked; packing up meanwhile all the gold and preciosities accumulated there (not forgetting Thor's illustrious gold collar, of which we shall hear again), and victoriously took the plunder home with him for his own royal uses and behoof of the state. In other cases, though a friend to strong measures, he had to hold in, and await the favorable moment. Thus once, in beginning a parliamentary address, so soon as he came to touch upon Christianity, the Bonders rose in murmurs, in vociferations and jingling of arms, which quite drowned the royal voice; declared, they had taken arms against king Hakon the Good to compel him to desist from his Christian proposals; and they did not think King Olaf a higher man than him (Hakon the Good). The king then said, "He purposed coming to them next Yule to their great sacrificial feast, to see for himself what their customs were," which pacified the Bonders for this time. The appointed place of meeting was again a Hakon–Jarl Temple, not yet done to ruin; chief shrine in those Trondhjem parts, I believe : there should Tryggveson appear at Yule. Well, but before Yule came, Tryggveson made a great banquet in his palace at Trondhjem, and invited far and wide, all manner of important persons out of the district as guests there. Banquet hardly done, Tryggveson gave some slight signal, upon which armed men strode in, seized eleven of these principal persons, and the king said: "Since he himself was to become a heathen again, and do sacrifice, it was his purpose to do it in the highest form, namely, that of Human Sacrifice; and this time not of slaves and malefactors, but of the best men in the country!" In which stringent circumstances the eleven seized persons, and company at large, gave unanimous consent to baptism; straightway received the same, and abjured their idols; but were not permitted to go home till they had left, in sons, brothers, and other precious relatives, sufficient hostages in the king's hands.

By unwearied industry of this and better kinds, Tryggveson had trampled down idolatry, so far as form went,—how far in substance may be greatly doubted. But it is to be remembered withal, that always on the back of these compulsory adventures there followed English bishops, priests and preachers; whereby to the open–minded, conviction, to all degrees of it, was attainable, while silence and passivity became the duty or necessity of the unconvinced party.

In about two years Norway was all gone over with a rough harrow of conversion. Heathenism at least constrained to be silent and outwardly conformable. Tryggveson, next turned his attention to Iceland, sent one Thangbrand, priest from Saxony, of wonderful qualities, military as well as theological, to try and convert Iceland.

25

Thangbrand made a few converts; for Olaf had already many estimable Iceland friends, whom he liked much, and was much liked by; and conversion was the ready road to his favor. Thangbrand, I find, lodged with Hall of Sida (familiar acquaintance of "Burnt Njal," whose Saga has its admirers among us even now). Thangbrand converted Hall and one or two other leading men,; but in general he was reckoned quarrelsome and blusterous rather than eloquent and piously convincing. Two skalds of repute made biting lampoons upon Thangbrand, whom Thangbrand, by two opportunities that offered, cut down and did to death because of their skaldic quality. Another he killed with his own hand, I know not for what reason. In brief, after about a year, Thangbrand returned to Norway and king Olaf; declaring the Icelanders to be a perverse, satirical, and inconvertible people, having himself, the record says, "been the death of three men there." King Olaf was in high rage at this result; but was persuaded by the Icelanders about him to try farther, and by a wilder instrument. He accordingly chose one Thormod, a pious, patient, and kindly man, who, within the next year or so, did actually accomplish the matter; namely, get Christianity, by open vote, declared at Thingvalla by the general Thing of Iceland there; the roar of a big thunder–clap at the right moment rather helping the conclusion, if I recollect. Whereupon Olaf's joy was no doubt great.

One general result of these successful operations was the discontent, to all manner of degrees, on the part of many Norse individuals, against this glorious and victorious, but peremptory and terrible king of theirs. Tryggveson, I fancy, did not much regard all that; a man of joyful, cheery temper, habitually contemptuous of danger. Another trivial misfortune that befell in these conversion operations, and became important to him, he did not even know of, and would have much despised if he had. It was this: Sigrid, queen dowager of Sweden, thought to be amongst the most shining women of the world, was also known for one of the most imperious, revengeful, and relentless, and had got for herself the name of Sigrid the Proud. In her high widowhood she had naturally many wooers; but treated them in a manner unexampled. Two of her suitors, a simultaneous Two, were, King Harald Graenske (a cousin of King Tryggveson's, and kind of king in some district, by sufferance of the late Hakon's),—this luckless Graenske and the then Russian Sovereign as well, name not worth mentioning, were zealous suitors of Queen Dowager Sigrid, and were perversely slow to accept the negative, which in her heart was inexorable for both, though the expression of it could not be quite so emphatic. By ill–luck for them they came once,—from the far West, Graenske; from the far East, the Russian;—and arrived both together at Sigrid's court, to prosecute their importunate, and to her odious and tiresome suit; much, how very much, to her impatience and disdain.

She lodged them both in some old mansion, which she had contiguous, and got compendiously furnished for them; and there, I know not whether on the first or on the second, or on what following night, this unparalleled Queen Sigrid had the house surrounded, set on fire, and the two suitors and their people burnt to ashes! No more of bother from these two at least! This appears to be a fact; and it could not be unknown to Tryggveson.

In spite of which, however, there went from Tryggveson, who was now a widower, some incipient marriage proposals to this proud widow; by whom they were favorably received; as from the brightest man in all the world, they might seem worth being. Now, in one of these anti—heathen onslaughts of King Olaf's on the idol temples of Hakon—(I think it was that case where Olaf's own battle—axe struck down the monstrous refulgent Thor, and conquered an immense gold ring from the neck of him, or from the door of his temple),—a huge gold ring, at any rate, had come into Olaf's hands; and this he bethought him might be a pretty present to Queen Sigrid, the now favorable, though the proud. Sigrid received the ring with joy; fancied what a collar it would make for her own fair neck; but noticed that her two goldsmiths, weighing it on their fingers, exchanged a glance. "What is that?" exclaimed Queen Sigrid. "Nothing," answered they, or endeavored to answer, dreading mischief. But Sigrid compelled them to break open the ring; and there was found, all along the inside of it, an occult ring of copper, not a heart of gold at all! "Ha," said the proud Queen, flinging it away, "he that could deceive in this matter can deceive in many others!" And was in hot wrath with Olaf; though, by degrees, again she took milder thoughts.

Milder thoughts, we say; and consented to a meeting next autumn, at some half—way station, where their great business might be brought to a happy settlement and betrothment. Both Olaf Tryggveson and the high dowager appear to have been tolerably of willing mind at this meeting; but Olaf interposed, what was always one condition with him, "Thou must consent to baptism, and give up thy idol—gods." "They are the gods of all my forefathers," answered the lady, "choose thou what gods thou pleasest, but leave me mine." Whereupon an altercation; and Tryggveson, as was his wont, towered up into shining wrath, and exclaimed at last, "Why should I care about thee then, old faded heathen creature?" And impatiently wagging his glove, hit her, or slightly switched her, on the face with it, and contemptuously turning away, walked out of the adventure. "This is a feat that may cost thee dear one day," said Sigrid. And in the end it came to do so, little as the magnificent Olaf deigned to think of it at the moment.

27

Early Kings of Norway

One of the last scuffles I remember of Olaf's having with his refractory heathens, was at a Thing in Hordaland or Rogaland, far in the North, where the chief opposition hero was one Jaernskaegg ("ironbeard") Scottice ("Airn–shag," as it were!). Here again was a grand heathen temple, Hakon Jarl's building, with a splendid Thor in it and much idol furniture. The king stated what was his constant wish here as elsewhere, but had no sooner entered upon the subject of Christianity than universal murmur, rising into clangor and violent dissent, interrupted him, and Ironbeard took up the discourse in reply. Ironbeard did not break down; on the contrary, he, with great brevity, emphasis, and clearness, signified "that the proposal to reject their old gods was in the highest degree unacceptable to this Thing; that it was contrary to bargain, withal; so that if it were insisted on, they would have to fight with the king about it; and in fact were now ready to do so." In reply to this, Olaf, without word uttered, but merely with some signal to the trusty armed men he had with him, rushed off to the temple close at hand; burst into it, shutting the door behind him; smashed Thor and Co. to destruction; then reappearing victorious, found much confusion outside, and, in particular, what was a most important item, the rugged Ironbeard done to death by Olaf's men in the interim. Which entirely disheartened the Thing from fighting at that moment; having now no leader who dared to head them in so dangerous an enterprise. So that every one departed to digest his rage in silence as he could.

Matters having cooled for a week or two, there was another Thing held; in which King Olaf testified regret for the quarrel that had fallen out, readiness to pay what *mulct* was due by law for that unlucky homicide of Ironbeard by his people; and, withal, to take the fair daughter of Ironbeard to wife, if all would comply and be friends with him in other matters; which was the course resolved on as most convenient: accept baptism, we; marry Jaernskaegg's daughter, you. This bargain held on both sides. The wedding, too, was celebrated, but that took rather a strange turn. On the morning of the bride–night, Olaf, who had not been sleeping, though his fair partner thought he had, opened his eyes, and saw, with astonishment, the fair partner aiming a long knife ready to strike home upon him! Which at once ended their wedded life; poor Demoiselle Ironbeard immediately bundling off with her attendants home again; King Olaf into the apartment of his servants, mentioning there what had happened, and forbidding any of them to follow her.

Olaf Tryggveson, though his kingdom was the smallest of the Norse Three, had risen to a renown over all the Norse world, which neither he of Denmark nor he of Sweden could pretend to rival. A magnificent, far–shining man; more expert in all "bodily exercises" as

28

the Norse call them, than any man had ever been before him, or after was. Could keep five daggers in the air, always catching the proper fifth by its handle, and sending it aloft again; could shoot supremely, throw a javelin with either hand; and, in fact, in battle usually throw two together. These, with swimming, climbing, leaping, were the then admirable Fine Arts of the North; in all which Tryggveson appears to have been the Raphael and the Michael Angelo at once. Essentially definable, too, if we look well into him, as a wild bit of real heroism, in such rude guise and environment; a high, true, and great human soul. A jovial burst of laughter in him, withal; a bright, airy, wise way of speech; dressed beautifully and with care; a man admired and loved exceedingly by those he liked; dreaded as death by those he did not like. "Hardly any king," says Snorro, "was ever so well obeyed; by one class out of zeal and love, by the rest out of dread." His glorious course, however, was not to last long.

King Svein of the Double−Beard had not yet completed his conquest of England,—by no means yet, some thirteen horrid years of that still before him!—when, over in Denmark, he found that complaints against him and intricacies had arisen, on the part principally of one Burislav, King of the Wends (far up the Baltic), and in a less degree with the King of Sweden and other minor individuals. Svein earnestly applied himself to settle these, and have his hands free. Burislav, an aged heathen gentleman, proved reasonable and conciliatory; so, too, the King of Sweden, and Dowager Queen Sigrid, his managing mother. Bargain in both these cases got sealed and crowned by marriage. Svein, who had become a widower lately, now wedded Sigrid; and might think, possibly enough, he had got a proud bargain, though a heathen one. Burislav also insisted on marriage with Princess Thyri, the Double−Beard's sister. Thyri, inexpressibly disinclined to wed an aged heathen of that stamp, pleaded hard with her brother; but the Double−Bearded was inexorable; Thyri's wailings and entreaties went for nothing. With some guardian foster−brother, and a serving−maid or two, she had to go on this hated journey. Old Burislav, at sight of her, blazed out into marriage−feast of supreme magnificence, and was charmed to see her; but Thyri would not join the marriage party; refused to eat with it or sit with it at all. Day after day, for six days, flatly refused; and after nightfall of the sixth, glided out with her foster−brother into the woods, into by−paths and inconceivable wanderings; and, in effect, got home to Denmark. Brother Svein was not for the moment there; probably enough gone to England again. But Thyri knew too well he would not allow her to stay here, or anywhere that he could help, except with the old heathen she had just fled from.

Thyri, looking round the world, saw no likely road for her, but to Olaf Tryggveson in Norway; to beg protection from the most heroic man she knew of in the world. Olaf, except by renown, was not known to her; but by renown he well was. Olaf, at sight of her, promised protection and asylum against all mortals. Nay, in discoursing with Thyri Olaf perceived more and more clearly what a fine handsome being, soul and body, Thyri was; and in a short space of time winded up by proposing marriage to Thyri; who, humbly, and we may fancy with what secret joy, consented to say yes, and become Queen of Norway. In the due months they had a little son, Harald; who, it is credibly recorded, was the joy of both his parents; but who, to their inexpressible sorrow, in about a year died, and vanished from them. This, and one other fact now to be mentioned, is all the wedded history we have of Thyri.

The other fact is, that Thyri had, by inheritance or covenant, not depending on her marriage with old Burislav, considerable properties in Wendland; which, she often reflected, might be not a little behooveful to her here in Norway, where her civil–list was probably but straitened. She spoke of this to her husband; but her husband would take no hold, merely made her gifts, and said, "Pooh, pooh, can't we live without old Burislav and his Wendland properties?" So that the lady sank into ever deeper anxiety and eagerness about this Wendland object; took to weeping; sat weeping whole days; and when Olaf asked, "What ails thee, then?" would answer, or did answer once, "What a different man my father Harald Gormson was [vulgarly called Blue–tooth], compared with some that are now kings! For no King Svein in the world would Harald Gormson have given up his own or his wife's just rights!" Whereupon Tryggveson started up, exclaiming in some heat, "Of thy brother Svein I never was afraid; if Svein and I meet in contest, it will not be Svein, I believe, that conquers;" and went off in a towering fume. Consented, however, at last, had to consent, to get his fine fleet equipped and armed, and decide to sail with it to Wendland to have speech and settlement with King Burislav.

Tryggveson had already ships and navies that were the wonder of the North. Especially in building war ships, the Crane, the Serpent, last of all the Long Serpent,[7]—he had, for size, for outward beauty, and inward perfection of equipment, transcended all example.

This new sea expedition became an object of attention to all neighbors; especially Queen Sigrid the Proud and Svein Double–Beard, her now king, were attentive to it.

Early Kings of Norway

"This insolent Tryggveson," Queen Sigrid would often say, and had long been saying, to her Svein, "to marry thy sister without leave had or asked of thee; and now flaunting forth his war navies, as if he, king only of paltry Norway, were the big hero of the North! Why do you suffer it, you kings really great?"

By such persuasions and reiterations, King Svein of Denmark, King Olaf of Sweden, and Jarl Eric, now a great man there, grown rich by prosperous sea robbery and other good management, were brought to take the matter up, and combine strenuously for destruction of King Olaf Tryggveson on this grand Wendland expedition of his. Fleets and forces were with best diligence got ready; and, withal, a certain Jarl Sigwald, of Jomsburg, chieftain of the Jomsvikings, a powerful, plausible, and cunning man, was appointed to find means of joining himself to Tryggveson's grand voyage, of getting into Tryggveson's confidence, and keeping Svein Double–Beard, Eric, and the Swedish King aware of all his movements.

King Olaf Tryggveson, unacquainted with all this, sailed away in summer, with his splendid fleet; went through the Belts with prosperous winds, under bright skies, to the admiration of both shores. Such a fleet, with its shining Serpents, long and short, and perfection of equipment and appearance, the Baltic never saw before. Jarl Sigwald joined with new ships by the way: "Had," he too, "a visit to King Burislav to pay; how could he ever do it in better company?" and studiously and skilfully ingratiated himself with King Olaf. Old Burislav, when they arrived, proved altogether courteous, handsome, and amenable; agreed at once to Olaf's claims for his now queen, did the rites of hospitality with a generous plenitude to Olaf; who cheerily renewed acquaintance with that country, known to him in early days (the cradle of his fortunes in the viking line), and found old friends there still surviving, joyful to meet him again. Jarl Sigwald encouraged these delays, King Svein and Co. not being yet quite ready. "Get ready!" Sigwald directed them, and they diligently did. Olaf's men, their business now done, were impatient to be home; and grudged every day of loitering there; but, till Sigwald pleased, such his power of flattering and cajoling Tryggveson, they could not get away.

At length, Sigwald's secret messengers reporting all ready on the part of Svein and Co., Olaf took farewell of Burislav and Wendland, and all gladly sailed away. Svein, Eric, and the Swedish king, with their combined fleets, lay in wait behind some cape in a safe little bay of some island, then called Svolde, but not in our time to be found; the Baltic tumults in the fourteenth century having swallowed it, as some think, and leaving us uncertain whether it was in the neighborhood of Rugen Island or in the Sound of Elsinore. There lay Svein, Eric, and Co. waiting till Tryggveson and his fleet came up, Sigwald's spy messengers daily reporting what progress he and it had made. At length, one bright summer morning, the fleet made appearance, sailing in loose order, Sigwald, as one acquainted with the shoal places, steering ahead, and showing them the way.

Snorro rises into one of his pictorial fits, seized with enthusiasm at the thought of such a fleet, and reports to us largely in what order Tryggveson's winged Coursers of the Deep, in long series, for perhaps an hour or more, came on, and what the three potentates, from their knoll of vantage, said of each as it hove in sight, Svein thrice over guessed this and the other noble vessel to be the Long Serpent; Eric, always correcting him, "No, that is not the Long Serpent yet" (and aside always), "Nor shall you be lord of it, king, when it does come." The Long Serpent itself did make appearance. Eric, Svein, and the Swedish king hurried on board, and pushed out of their hiding–place into the open sea. Treacherous Sigwald, at the beginning of all this, had suddenly doubled that cape of theirs, and struck into the bay out of sight, leaving the foremost Tryggveson ships astonished, and uncertain what to do, if it were not simply to strike sail and wait till Olaf himself with the Long Serpent arrived.

Olaf's chief captains, seeing the enemy's huge fleet come out, and how the matter lay, strongly advised King Olaf to elude this stroke of treachery, and, with all sail, hold on his course, fight being now on so unequal terms. Snorro says, the king, high on the quarter–deck where he stood, replied, "Strike the sails; never shall men of mine think of flight. I never fled from battle. Let God dispose of my life; but flight I will never take." And so the battle arrangements immediately began, and the battle with all fury went loose; and lasted hour after hour, till almost sunset, if I well recollect. "Olaf stood on the Serpent's quarter–deck," says Snorro, "high over the others. He had a gilt shield and a helmet inlaid with gold; over his armor he had a short red coat, and was easily distinguished from other men." Snorro's account of the battle is altogether animated, graphic, and so minute that antiquaries gather from it, if so disposed (which we but little are), what the methods of Norse sea–fighting were; their shooting of arrows, casting of javelins, pitching of big stones, ultimately boarding, and mutual clashing and smashing, which it would not avail us to speak of here. Olaf stood conspicuous all day, throwing javelins, of deadly aim, with both hands at once; encouraging, fighting and commanding like a highest sea–king.

The Danish fleet, the Swedish fleet, were, both of them, quickly dealt with, and successively withdrew out of shot-range. And then Jarl Eric came up, and fiercely grappled with the Long Serpent, or, rather, with her surrounding comrades; and gradually, as they were beaten empty of men, with the Long Serpent herself. The fight grew ever fiercer, more furious. Eric was supplied with new men from the Swedes and Danes; Olaf had no such resource, except from the crews of his own beaten ships, and at length this also failed him; all his ships, except the Long Serpent, being beaten and emptied. Olaf fought on unyielding. Eric twice boarded him, was twice repulsed. Olaf kept his quarterdeck; unconquerable, though left now more and more hopeless, fatally short of help. A tall young man, called Einar Tamberskelver, very celebrated and important afterwards in Norway, and already the best archer known, kept busy with his bow. Twice he nearly shot Jarl Eric in his ship. "Shoot me that man," said Jarl Eric to a bowman near him; and, just as Tamberskelver was drawing his bow the third time, an arrow hit it in the middle and broke it in two. "What is this that has broken?" asked King Olaf. "Norway from thy hand, king," answered Tamberskelver. Tryggveson's men, he observed with surprise, were striking violently on Eric's; but to no purpose: nobody fell. "How is this?" asked Tryggveson. "Our swords are notched and blunted, king; they do not cut." Olaf stept down to his arm-chest; delivered out new swords; and it was observed as he did it, blood ran trickling from his wrist; but none knew where the wound was. Eric boarded a third time. Olaf, left with hardly more than one man, sprang overboard (one sees that red coat of his still glancing in the evening sun), and sank in the deep waters to his long rest.

Rumor ran among his people that he still was not dead; grounding on some movement by the ships of that traitorous Sigwald, they fancied Olaf had dived beneath the keels of his enemies, and got away with Sigwald, as Sigwald himself evidently did. "Much was hoped, supposed, spoken," says one old mourning Skald; "but the truth was, Olaf Tryggveson was never seen in Norseland more." Strangely he remains still a shining figure to us; the wildly beautifulest man, in body and in soul, that one has ever heard of in the North.

CHAPTER VIII. JARLS ERIC AND SVEIN.

Jarl Eric, splendent with this victory, not to speak of that over the Jomsburgers with his father long ago, was now made Governor of Norway: Governor or quasi-sovereign, with his brother, Jarl. Svein, as partner, who, however, took but little hand in governing;—and, under the patronage of Svein Double–Beard and the then Swedish king (Olaf his name, Sigrid the Proud, his mother's), administered it, they say, with skill and prudence for above fourteen years. Tryggveson's death is understood and laboriously computed to have happened in the year 1000; but there is no exact chronology in these things, but a continual uncertain guessing after such; so that one eye in History as regards them is as if put out;—neither indeed have I yet had the luck to find any decipherable and intelligible map of Norway: so that the other eye of History is much blinded withal, and her path through those wild regions and epochs is an extremely dim and chaotic one. An evil that much demands remedying, and especially wants some first attempt at remedying, by inquirers into English History; the whole period from Egbert, the first Saxon King of England, on to Edward the Confessor, the last, being everywhere completely interwoven with that of their mysterious, continually invasive "Danes," as they call them, and inextricably unintelligible till these also get to be a little understood, and cease to be utterly dark, hideous, and mythical to us as they now are.

King Olaf Tryggveson is the first Norseman who is expressly mentioned to have been in England by our English History books, new or old; and of him it is merely said that he had an interview with King Ethelred II. at Andover, of a pacific and friendly nature,—though it is absurdly added that the noble Olaf was converted to Christianity by that extremely stupid Royal Person. Greater contrast in an interview than in this at Andover, between heroic Olaf Tryggveson and Ethelred the forever Unready, was not perhaps seen in the terrestrial Planet that day. Olaf or "Olaus," or "Anlaf," as they name him, did "engage on oath to Ethelred not to invade England any more," and kept his promise, they farther say. Essentially a truth, as we already know, though the circumstances were all different; and the promise was to a devout High Priest, not to a crowned Blockhead and cowardly Do–nothing. One other "Olaus" I find mentioned in our Books, two or three centuries before, at a time when there existed no such individual; not to speak of several Anlafs, who sometimes seem to mean Olaf and still oftener to mean nobody possible. Which occasions not a little obscurity in our early History, says the learned Selden. A thing remediable, too, in which, if any Englishman of due genius (or even capacity for standing labor), who understood the Icelandic and Anglo–Saxon languages, would engage in it, he might do a great deal of good, and bring the matter into a comparatively lucid state. Vain aspirations,—or perhaps not altogether vain.

Early Kings of Norway

At the time of Olaf Tryggveson's death, and indeed long before, King Svein Double-Beard had always for chief enterprise the Conquest of England, and followed it by fits with extreme violence and impetus; often advancing largely towards a successful conclusion; but never, for thirteen years yet, getting it concluded. He possessed long since all England north of Watling Street. That is to say, Northumberland, East Anglia (naturally full of Danish settlers by this time), were fixedly his; Mercia, his oftener than not; Wessex itself, with all the coasts, he was free to visit, and to burn and rob in at discretion. There or elsewhere, Ethelred the Unready had no battle in him whatever; and, for a forty years after the beginning of his reign, England excelled in anarchic stupidity, murderous devastation, utter misery, platitude, and sluggish contemptibility, all the countries one has read of. Apparently a very opulent country, too; a ready skill in such arts and fine arts as there were; Svein's very ships, they say, had their gold dragons, top-mast pennons, and other metallic splendors generally wrought for them in England. "Unexampled prosperity" in the manufacture way not unknown there, it would seem! But co-existing with such spiritual bankruptcy as was also unexampled, one would hope. Read Lupus (Wulfstan), Archbishop of York's amazing *Sermon* on the subject,[8] addressed to contemporary audiences; setting forth such a state of things,—sons selling their fathers, mothers, and sisters as Slaves to the Danish robber; themselves living in debauchery, blusterous gluttony, and depravity; the details of which are well-nigh incredible, though clearly stated as things generally known,—the humor of these poor wretches sunk to a state of what we may call greasy desperation, "Let us eat and drink, for to-morrow we die." The manner in which they treated their own English nuns, if young, good-looking, and captive to the Danes; buying them on a kind of brutish or subter-brutish "Greatest Happiness Principle" (for the moment), and by a Joint-Stock arrangement, far transcends all human speech or imagination, and awakens in one the momentary red-hot thought, The Danes have served you right, ye accursed! The so-called soldiers, one finds, made not the least fight anywhere; could make none, led and guided as they were, and the "Generals" often enough traitors, always ignorant, and blockheads, were in the habit, when expressly commanded to fight, of taking physic, and declaring that nature was incapable of castor-oil and battle both at once. This ought to be explained a little to the modern English and their War-Secretaries, who undertake the conduct of armies. The undeniable fact is, defeat on defeat was the constant fate of the English; during these forty years not one battle in which they were not beaten. No gleam of victory or real resistance till the noble Edmund Ironside (whom it is always strange to me how such an Ethelred could produce for son) made his appearance and ran his brief course, like a great and far-seen meteor, soon extinguished without result. No remedy for

35

England in that base time, but yearly asking the victorious, plundering, burning and murdering Danes, "How much money will you take to go away?" Thirty thousand pounds in silver, which the annual Danegelt soon rose to, continued to be about the average yearly sum, though generally on the increasing hand; in the last year I think it had risen to seventy–two thousand pounds in silver, raised yearly by a tax (Income–tax of its kind, rudely levied), the worst of all remedies, good for the day only. Nay, there was one remedy still worse, which the miserable Ethelred once tried: that of massacring "all the Danes settled in England" (practically, of a few thousands or hundreds of them), by treachery and a kind of Sicilian Vespers. Which issued, as such things usually do, in terrible monition to you not to try the like again! Issued, namely, in redoubled fury on the Danish part; new fiercer invasion by Svein's Jarl Thorkel; then by Svein himself; which latter drove the miserable Ethelred, with wife and family, into Normandy, to wife's brother, the then Duke there; and ended that miserable struggle by Svein's becoming King of England himself. Of this disgraceful massacre, which it would appear has been immensely exaggerated in the English books, we can happily give the exact date (A.D. 1002); and also of Svein's victorious accession (A.D. 1013),[9]—pretty much the only benefit one gets out of contemplating such a set of objects.

King Svein's first act was to levy a terribly increased Income–Tax for the payment of his army. Svein was levying it with a stronghanded diligence, but had not yet done levying it, when, at Gainsborough one night, he suddenly died; smitten dead, once used to be said, by St. Edmund, whilom murdered King of the East Angles; who could not bear to see his shrine and monastery of St. Edmundsbury plundered by the Tyrant's tax–collectors, as they were on the point of being. In all ways impossible, however,—Edmund's own death did not occur till two years after Svein's. Svein's death, by whatever cause, befell 1014; his fleet, then lying in the Humber; and only Knut,[10] his eldest son (hardly yet eighteen, count some), in charge of it; who, on short counsel, and arrangement about this questionable kingdom of his, lifted anchor; made for Sandwich, a safer station at the moment; "cut off the feet and noses" (one shudders, and hopes not, there being some discrepancy about it!) of his numerous hostages that had been delivered to King Svein; set them ashore;—and made for Denmark, his natural storehouse and stronghold, as the hopefulest first thing he could do.

Knut soon returned from Denmark, with increase of force sufficient for the English problem; which latter he now ended in a victorious, and essentially, for himself and chaotic England, beneficent manner. Became widely known by and by, there and elsewhere, as Knut the Great; and is thought by judges of our day to have really merited that title. A most nimble, sharp–striking, clear–thinking, prudent and effective man, who regulated this dismembered and distracted England in its Church matters, in its State matters, like a real King. Had a Standing Army (House Carles), who were well paid, well drilled and disciplined, capable of instantly quenching insurrection or breakage of the peace; and piously endeavored (with a signal earnestness, and even devoutness, if we look well) to do justice to all men, and to make all men rest satisfied with justice. In a word, he successfully strapped up, by every true method and regulation, this miserable, dislocated, and dissevered mass of bleeding Anarchy into something worthy to be called an England again;—only that he died too soon, and a second "Conqueror" of us, still weightier of structure, and under improved auspices, became possible, and was needed here! To appearance, Knut himself was capable of being a Charlemagne of England and the North (as has been already said or quoted), had he only lived twice as long as he did. But his whole sum of years seems not to have exceeded forty. His father Svein of the Forkbeard is reckoned to have been fifty to sixty when St. Edmund finished him at Gainsborough. We now return to Norway, ashamed of this long circuit which has been a truancy more or less.

CHAPTER IX. KING OLAF THE THICK–SET'S VIKING DAYS.

King Harald Graenske, who, with another from Russia accidentally lodging beside him, got burned to death in Sweden, courting that unspeakable Sigrid the Proud,—was third cousin or so to Tryggve, father of our heroic Olaf. Accurately counted, he is great–grandson of Bjorn the Chapman, first of Haarfagr's sons whom Eric Bloodaxe made away with. His little "kingdom," as he called it, was a district named the Greenland (Graeneland); he himself was one of those little Haarfagr kinglets whom Hakon Jarl, much more Olaf Tryggveson, was content to leave reigning, since they would keep the peace with him. Harald had a loving wife of his own, Aasta the name of her, soon expecting the birth of her and his pretty babe, named Olaf,—at the time he went on that deplorable Swedish adventure, the foolish, fated creature, and ended self and kingdom altogether. Aasta was greatly shocked; composed herself however; married a new husband, Sigurd Syr, a kinglet, and a great–grandson of Harald Fairhair, a man of great wealth, prudence, and influence in those countries; in whose house, as favorite and well–beloved stepson, little Olaf was wholesomely and skilfully brought up. In Sigurd's house he had, withal, a special tutor entertained for him, one Rane, known as Rane the

Far–travelled, by whom he could be trained, from the earliest basis, in Norse accomplishments and arts. New children came, one or two; but Olaf, from his mother, seems always to have known that he was the distinguished and royal article there. One day his Foster–father, hurrying to leave home on business, hastily bade Olaf, no other being by, saddle his horse for him. Olaf went out with the saddle, chose the biggest he–goat about, saddled that, and brought it to the door by way of horse. Old Sigurd, a most grave man, grinned sardonically at the sight. "Hah, I see thou hast no mind to take commands from me; thou art of too high a humor to take commands." To which, says Snorro, Boy Olaf answered little except by laughing, till Sigurd saddled for himself, and rode away. His mother Aasta appears to have been a thoughtful, prudent woman, though always with a fierce royalism at the bottom of her memory, and a secret implacability on that head.

At the age of twelve Olaf went to sea; furnished with a little fleet, and skilful sea–counsellor, expert old Rane, by his Foster–father, and set out to push his fortune in the world. Rane was a steersman and counsellor in these incipient times; but the crew always called Olaf "King," though at first, as Snorro thinks, except it were in the hour of battle, he merely pulled an oar. He cruised and fought in this capacity on many seas and shores; passed several years, perhaps till the age of nineteen or twenty, in this wild element and way of life; fighting always in a glorious and distinguished manner. In the hour of battle, diligent enough "to amass property," as the Vikings termed it; and in the long days and nights of sailing, given over, it is likely, to his own thoughts and the unfathomable dialogue with the ever–moaning Sea; not the worst High School a man could have, and indeed infinitely preferable to the most that are going even now, for a high and deep young soul.

His first distinguished expedition was to Sweden: natural to go thither first, to avenge his poor father's death, were it nothing more. Which he did, the Skalds say, in a distinguished manner; making victorious and handsome battle for himself, in entering Maelare Lake; and in getting out of it again, after being frozen there all winter, showing still more surprising, almost miraculous contrivance and dexterity. This was the first of his glorious victories, of which the Skalds reckon up some fourteen or thirteen very glorious indeed, mostly in the Western and Southern countries, most of all in England; till the name of Olaf Haraldson became quite famous in the Viking and strategic world. He seems really to have learned the secrets of his trade, and to have been, then and afterwards, for vigilance, contrivance, valor, and promptitude of execution, a superior fighter. Several exploits recorded of him betoken, in simple forms, what may be called a military genius.

The principal, and to us the alone interesting, of his exploits seem to have lain in England, and, what is further notable, always on the anti–Svein side. English books do not mention him at all that I can find; but it is fairly credible that, as the Norse records report, in the end of Ethelred's reign, he was the ally or hired general of Ethelred, and did a great deal of sea–fighting, watching, sailing, and sieging for this miserable king and Edmund Ironside, his son. Snorro says expressly, London, the impregnable city, had to be besieged again for Ethelred's behoof (in the interval between Svein's death and young Knut's getting back from Denmark), and that our Olaf Haraldson was the great engineer and victorious captor of London on that singular occasion,—London captured for the first time. The Bridge, as usual, Snorro says, offered almost insuperable obstacles. But the engineering genius of Olaf contrived huge "platforms of wainscoting [old walls of wooden houses, in fact], bound together by withes;" these, carried steadily aloft above the ships, will (thinks Olaf) considerably secure them and us from the destructive missiles, big boulder stones, and other, mischief profusely showered down on us, till we get under the Bridge with axes and cables, and do some good upon it. Olaf's plan was tried; most of the other ships, in spite of their wainscoting and withes, recoiled on reaching the Bridge, so destructive were the boulder and other missile showers. But Olaf's ships and self got actually under the Bridge; fixed all manner of cables there; and then, with the river current in their favor, and the frightened ships rallying to help in this safer part of the enterprise, tore out the important piles and props, and fairly broke the poor Bridge, wholly or partly, down into the river, and its Danish defenders into immediate surrender. That is Snorro's account.

On a previous occasion, Olaf had been deep in a hopeful combination with Ethelred's two younger sons, Alfred and Edward, afterwards King Edward the Confessor: That they two should sally out from Normandy in strong force, unite with Olaf in ditto, and, landing on the Thames, do something effectual for themselves. But impediments, bad weather or the like, disheartened the poor Princes, and it came to nothing. Olaf was much in Normandy, what they then called Walland; a man held in honor by those Norman Dukes.

What amount of "property" he had amassed I do not know, but could prove, were it necessary, that he had acquired some tactical or even strategic faculty and real talent for war. At Lymfjord, in Jutland, but some years after this (A.D. 1027), he had a sea–battle with the great Knut himself,—ships combined with flood–gates, with roaring, artificial deluges; right well managed by King Olaf; which were within a hair's–breadth of destroying Knut, now become a King and Great; and did in effect send him instantly running. But of this more particularly by and by.

What still more surprises me is the mystery, where Olaf, in this wandering, fighting, sea–roving life, acquired his deeply religious feeling, his intense adherence to the Christian Faith. I suppose it had been in England, where many pious persons, priestly and other, were still to be met with, that Olaf had gathered these doctrines; and that in those his unfathomable dialogues with the ever–moaning Ocean, they had struck root downwards in the soul of him, and borne fruit upwards to the degree so conspicuous afterwards. It is certain he became a deeply pious man during these long Viking cruises; and directed all his strength, when strength and authority were lent him, to establishing the Christian religion in his country, and suppressing and abolishing Vikingism there; both of which objects, and their respective worth and unworth, he, must himself have long known so well.

It was well on in A.D. 1016 that Knut gained his last victory, at Ashdon, in Essex, where the earth pyramids and antique church near by still testify the thankful piety of Knut,—or, at lowest his joy at having *won* instead of lost and perished, as he was near doing there. And it was still this same year when the noble Edmund Ironside, after forced partition–treaty "in the Isle of Alney," got scandalously murdered, and Knut became indisputable sole King of England, and decisively settled himself to his work of governing there. In the year before either of which events, while all still hung uncertain for Knut, and even Eric Jarl of Norway had to be summoned in aid of him, in that year 1015, as one might naturally guess and as all Icelandic hints and indications lead us to date the thing, Olaf had decided to give up Vikingism in all its forms; to return to Norway, and try whether he could not assert the place and career that belonged to him there. Jarl Eric had vanished with all his war forces towards England, leaving only a boy, Hakon, as successor, and Svein, his own brother,—a quiet man, who had always avoided war. Olaf landed in Norway without obstacle; but decided to be quiet till he had himself examined and consulted friends.

His reception by his mother Aasta was of the kindest and proudest, and is lovingly described by Snorro. A pretty idyllic, or epic piece, of Norse Homeric type: How Aasta, hearing of her son's advent, set all her maids and menials to work at the top of their speed; despatched a runner to the harvest–field, where her husband Sigurd was, to warn him to come home and dress. How Sigurd was standing among his harvest folk, reapers and binders; and what he had on,—broad slouch hat, with veil (against the midges), blue kirtle, hose of I forget what color, with laced boots; and in his hand a stick with silver head and ditto ring upon it;—a personable old gentleman, of the eleventh century, in those parts. Sigurd was cautious, prudentially cunctatory, though heartily friendly in his counsel to Olaf as to the King question. Aasta had a Spartan tone in her wild maternal heart; and assures Olaf that she, with a half—reproachful glance at Sigurd, will stand by him to the death in this his just and noble enterprise. Sigurd promises to consult farther in his neighborhood, and to correspond by messages; the result is, Olaf resolutely pushing forward himself, resolves to call a Thing, and openly claim his kingship there. The Thing itself was willing enough: opposition parties do here and there bestir themselves; but Olaf is always swifter than they. Five kinglets somewhere in the Uplands,[11]—all descendants of Haarfagr; but averse to break the peace, which Jarl Eric and Hakon Jarl both have always willingly allowed to peaceable people,—seem to be the main opposition party. These five take the field against Olaf with what force they have; Olaf, one night, by beautiful celerity and strategic practice which a Friedrich or a Turenne might have approved, surrounds these Five; and when morning breaks, there is nothing for them but either death, or else instant surrender, and swearing of fealty to King Olaf. Which latter branch of the alternative they gladly accept, the whole five of them, and go home again.

This was a beautiful bit of war—practice by King Olaf on land. By another stroke still more compendious at sea, he had already settled poor young Hakon, and made him peaceable for a long while. Olaf by diligent quest and spy—messaging, had ascertained that Hakon, just returning from Denmark and farewell to Papa and Knut, both now under way for England, was coasting north towards Trondhjem; and intended on or about such a day to land in such and such a fjord towards the end of this Trondhjem voyage. Olaf at once mans two big ships, steers through the narrow mouth of the said fjord, moors one ship on the north shore, another on the south; fixes a strong cable, well sunk under water, to the capstans of these two; and in all quietness waits for Hakon. Before many hours, Hakon's royal or quasi—royal barge steers gaily into this fjord; is a little surprised, perhaps, to see within the jaws of it two big ships at anchor, but steers gallantly along, nothing doubting. Olaf with a signal of "All hands," works his two capstans; has the cable up high enough at the right moment, catches with it the keel of poor Hakon's barge, upsets it, empties it wholly into the sea. Wholly into the sea; saves Hakon, however, and his people from drowning, and brings them on board. His dialogue with poor young

Hakon, especially poor young Hakon's responses, is very pretty. Shall I give it, out of Snorro, and let the reader take it for as authentic as he can? It is at least the true image of it in authentic Snorro's head, little more than two centuries later.

"Jarl Hakon was led up to the king's ship. He was the handsomest man that could be seen. He had long hair as fine as silk, bound about his head with a gold ornament. When he sat down in the forehold the king said to him:

King. "'It is not false, what is said of your family, that ye are handsome people to look at; but now your luck has deserted you.'

Hakon. "'It has always been the case that success is changeable; and there is no luck in the matter. It has gone with your family as with mine to have by turns the better lot. I am little beyond childhood in years; and at any rate we could not have defended ourselves, as we did not expect any attack on the way. It may turn out better with us another time.'

King. "'Dost thou not apprehend that thou art in such a condition that, hereafter, there can be neither victory nor defeat for thee?'

Hakon. "'That is what only thou canst determine, King, according to thy pleasure.'

King. "'What wilt thou give me, Jarl, if, for this time, I let thee go, whole and unhurt?'

Hakon. "'What wilt thou take, King?'

King. "'Nothing, except that thou shalt leave the country; give up thy kingdom; and take an oath that thou wilt never go into battle against me.'"[12]

Jarl Hakon accepted the generous terms; went to England and King Knut, and kept his bargain for a good few years; though he was at last driven, by pressure of King Knut, to violate it,—little to his profit, as we shall see. One victorious naval battle with Jarl Svein, Hakon's uncle, and his adherents, who fled to Sweden, after his beating,—battle not difficult to a skilful, hard–hitting king,—was pretty much all the actual fighting Olaf had to do in this enterprise. He various times met angry Bonders and refractory Things with arms in their hand; but by skilful, firm management,—perfectly patient, but also perfectly ready to be active,—he mostly managed without coming to strokes; and was universally recognized by Norway as its real king. A promising young man, and fit to be a king, thinks Snorro. Only of middle stature, almost rather shortish; but firm-standing, and stout-built; so that they got to call him Olaf the Thick (meaning Olaf the Thick-set, or Stout-built), though his final epithet among them was infinitely higher. For the rest, "a comely, earnest, prepossessing look; beautiful yellow hair in quantity; broad, honest face, of a complexion pure as snow and rose;" and finally (or firstly) "the brightest eyes in the world; such that, in his anger, no man could stand them." He had a heavy task ahead, and needed all his qualities and fine gifts to get it done.

CHAPTER X. REIGN OF KING OLAF THE SAINT.

The late two Jarls, now gone about their business, had both been baptized, and called themselves Christians. But during their government they did nothing in the conversion way; left every man to choose his own God or Gods; so that some had actually two, the Christian God by land, and at sea Thor, whom they considered safer in that element. And in effect the mass of the people had fallen back into a sluggish heathenism or half-heathenism, the life-labor of Olaf Tryggveson lying ruinous or almost quite overset. The new Olaf, son of Harald, set himself with all his strength to mend such a state of matters; and stood by his enterprise to the end, as the one highest interest, including all others, for his People and him. His method was by no means soft; on the contrary, it was hard, rapid, severe,—somewhat on the model of Tryggveson's, though with more of bishoping and preaching superadded. Yet still there was a great deal of mauling, vigorous punishing, and an entire intolerance of these two things: Heathenism and Sea-robbery, at least of Sea-robbery in the old style; whether in the style we moderns still practise, and call privateering, I do not quite know. But Vikingism proper had to cease in Norway; still more, Heathenism, under penalties too severe to he borne; death, mutilation of limb, not to mention forfeiture and less rigorous coercion. Olaf was inexorable against violation of the law. "Too severe," cried many; to whom one answers, "Perhaps in part yes, perhaps also in great part *no*; depends altogether on the previous question, How far the law was the eternal one of God Almighty in the universe, How far the law merely of Olaf (destitute of right inspiration) left to his own passions and whims?"

Many were the jangles Olaf had with the refractory Heathen Things and Ironbeards of a new generation: very curious to see. Scarcely ever did it come to fighting between King and Thing, though often enough near it; but the Thing discerning, as it usually did in time, that the King was stronger in men, seemed to say unanimously to itself, "We have lost, then; baptize us, we must burn our old gods and conform." One new feature we do slightly discern: here and there a touch of theological argument on the heathen side. At one wild Thing, far up in the Dovrefjeld, of a very heathen temper, there was much of that; not to be quenched by King Olaf at the moment; so that it had to be adjourned till the morrow, and again till the next day. Here are some traits of it, much abridged from Snorro (who gives a highly punctual account), which vividly represent Olaf's posture and manner of proceeding in such intricacies.

The chief Ironbeard on this occasion was one Gudbrand, a very rugged peasant; who, says Snorro, was like a king in that district. Some days before, King Olaf, intending a religious Thing in those deeply heathen parts, with alternative of Christianity or conflagration, is reported, on looking down into the valley and the beautiful village of Loar standing there, to have said wistfully, "What a pity it is that so beautiful a village should be burnt!" Olaf sent out his message–token all the, same, however, and met Gudbrand and an immense assemblage, whose humor towards him was uncompliant to a high degree indeed. Judge by this preliminary speech of Gudbrand to his Thing–people, while Olaf was not yet arrived, but only advancing, hardly got to Breeden on the other side of the hill: "A man has come to Loar who is called Olaf," said Gudbrand, "and will force upon us another faith than we had before, and will break in pieces all our Gods. He says he has a much greater and more powerful God; and it is wonderful that the earth does not burst asunder under him, or that our God lets him go about unpunished when he dares to talk such things. I know this for certain, that if we carry Thor, who has always stood by us, out of our Temple that is standing upon this farm, Olaf's God will melt away, and he and his men be made nothing as soon as Thor looks upon them." Whereupon the Bonders all shouted as one man, "Yea!"

Which tremendous message they even forwarded to Olaf, by Gudbrand's younger son at the head of 700 armed men; but did not terrify Olaf with it, who, on the contrary, drew up his troops, rode himself at the head of them, and began a speech to the Bonders, in which he invited them to adopt Christianity, as the one true faith for mortals.

Far from consenting to this, the Bonders raised a general shout, smiting at the same time their shields with their weapons; but Olaf's men advancing on them swiftly, and flinging spears, they turned and ran, leaving Gudbrand's son behind, a prisoner, to whom Olaf gave his life: "Go home now to thy father, and tell him I mean to be with him soon." The son goes accordingly, and advises his father not to face Olaf; but Gudbrand angrily replies: "Ha, coward! I see thou, too, art taken by the folly that man is going about with;" and is resolved to fight. That night, however, Gudbrand has a most remarkable Dream, or Vision: a Man surrounded by light, bringing great terror with him, who warns Gudbrand against doing battle with Olaf. "If thou dost, thou and all thy people will fall; wolves will drag away thee and thine; ravens will tear thee in stripes!" And lo, in telling this to Thord Potbelly, a sturdy neighbor of his and henchman in the Thing, it is found that to Thord also has come the self same terrible Apparition! Better propose truce to Olaf (who seems to have these dreadful Ghostly Powers on his side), and the holding of a Thing, to discuss matters between us. Thing assembles, on a day of heavy rain. Being all seated, uprises King Olaf, and informs them: "The people of Lesso, Loar, and Vaage, have accepted Christianity, and broken down their idol–houses: they believe now in the True God, who has made heaven and earth, and knows all things;" and sits down again without more words.

"Gudbrand replies, 'We know nothing about him of whom thou speakest. Dost thou call him God, whom neither thou nor any one else can see? But we have a God who can be seen every day, although he is not out to–day because the weather is wet; and he will appear to thee terrible and very grand; and I expect that fear will mix with thy very blood when he comes into the Thing. But since thou sayest thy God is so great, let him make it so that to–morrow we have a cloudy day, but without rain, and then let us meet again.'

"The king accordingly returned home to his lodging, taking Gudbrand's son as a hostage; but he gave them a man as hostage in exchange. In the evening the king asked Gudbrand's son What their God was like? He replied that he bore the likeness of Thor; had a hammer in his hand; was of great size, but hollow within; and had a high stand, upon which he stood when he was out. 'Neither gold nor silver are wanting about him, and every day he receives four cakes of bread, besides meat.' They then went to bed; but the king watched all night in prayer. When day dawned the king went to mass; then to table, and from thence to the Thing. The weather was such as Gudbrand desired. Now the Bishop stood up in his choir–robes, with bishop's coif on his head, and bishop's crosier in his hand. He spoke to the Bonders of the true faith, told the many wonderful acts of God, and concluded his speech well.

"Thord Potbelly replies, 'Many things we are told of by this learned man with the staff in his hand, crooked at the top like a ram's horn. But since you say, comrades, that your God

45

is so powerful, and can do so many wonders, tell him to make it clear sunshine to—morrow forenoon, and then we shall meet here again, and do one of two things,—either agree with you about this business, or fight you.' And they separated for the day."

Overnight the king instructed Kolbein the Strong, an immense fellow, the same who killed Gunhild's two brothers, that he, Kolbein, must stand next him to—morrow; people must go down to where the ships of the Bonders lay, and punctually bore holes in every one of them; item, to the farms where their horses wore, and punctually unhalter the whole of them, and let them loose: all which was done. Snorro continues:—

"Now the king was in prayer all night, beseeching God of his goodness and mercy to release him from evil. When mass was ended, and morning was gray, the king went to the Thing. When he came thither, some Bonders had already arrived, and they saw a great crowd coming along, and bearing among them a huge man's image, glancing with gold and silver. When the Bonders who were at the Thing saw it, they started up, and bowed themselves down before the ugly idol. Thereupon it was set down upon the Thing field; and on the one side of it sat the Bonders, and on the other the King and his people.

"Then Dale Gudbrand stood up and said, 'Where now, king, is thy God? I think he will now carry his head lower; and neither thou, nor the man with the horn, sitting beside thee there, whom thou callest Bishop, are so bold to—day as on the former days. For now our God, who rules over all, is come, and looks on you with an angry eye; and now I see well enough that you are terrified, and scarcely dare raise your eyes. Throw away now all your opposition, and believe in the God who has your fate wholly in his hands.'

"The king now whispers to Kolbein the Strong, without the Bonders perceiving it, 'If it come so in the course of my speech that the Bonders look another way than towards their idol, strike him as hard as thou canst with thy club.'

"The king then stood up and spoke. 'Much hast thou talked to us this morning, and greatly hast thou wondered that thou canst not see our God; but we expect that he will soon come to us. Thou wouldst frighten us with thy God, who is both blind and deaf, and cannot even move about without being carried; but now I expect it will be but a short time before he meets his fate: for turn your eyes towards the east,—behold our God advancing in great light.'

"The sun was rising, and all turned to look. At that moment Kolbein gave their God a stroke, so that he quite burst asunder; and there ran out of him mice as big almost as cats, and reptiles and adders. The Bonders were so terrified that some fled to their ships; but when they sprang out upon them the ships filled with water, and could not get away. Others ran to their horses, but could not find them. The king then ordered the Bonders to be called together, saying he wanted to speak with them; on which the Bonders came back, and the Thing was again seated.

"The king rose up and said, 'I do not understand what your noise and running mean. You yourselves see what your God can do,—the idol you adorned with gold and silver, and brought meat and provisions to. You see now that the protecting powers, who used and got good of all that, were the mice and adders, the reptiles and lizards; and surely they do ill who trust to such, and will not abandon this folly. Take now your gold and ornaments that are lying strewed on the grass, and give them to your wives and daughters, but never hang them hereafter upon stocks and stones. Here are two conditions between us to choose upon: either accept Christianity, or fight this very day, and the victory be to them to whom the God we worship gives it.'

"Then Dale Gudbrand stood up and said, 'We have sustained great damage upon our God; but since he will not help us, we will believe in the God whom thou believest in.'

"Then all received Christianity. The Bishop baptized Gudbrand and his son. King Olaf and Bishop Sigurd left behind them teachers; and they who met as enemies parted as friends. And afterwards Gudbrand built a church in the valley."[13]

Olaf was by no means an unmerciful man,—much the reverse where he saw good cause. There was a wicked old King Raerik, for example, one of those five kinglets whom, with their bits of armaments, Olaf by stratagem had surrounded one night, and at once bagged and subjected when morning rose, all of them consenting; all of them except this Raerik, whom Olaf, as the readiest sure course, took home with him; blinded, and kept in his own house; finding there was no alternative but that or death to the obstinate old dog, who was a kind of distant cousin withal, and could not conscientiously be killed. Stone-blind old Raerik was not always in murderous humor. Indeed, for most part he wore a placid, conciliatory aspect, and said shrewd amusing things; but had thrice over tried, with amazing cunning of contrivance, though stone-blind, to thrust a dagger into Olaf and the last time had all but succeeded. So that, as Olaf still refused to have him killed, it had become a problem what was to be done with him. Olaf's good humor, as well as *his* quiet, ready sense and practicality, are manifested in his final settlement of this Raerik problem. Olaf's laugh, I can perceive, was not so loud as Tryggveson's but equally hearty, coming from the bright mind of him!

Besides blind Raerik, Olaf had in his household one Thorarin, an Icelander; a remarkably ugly man, says Snorro, but a far–travelled, shrewdly observant, loyal–minded, and good–humored person, whom Olaf liked to talk with. "Remarkably ugly," says Snorro, "especially in his hands and feet, which were large and ill–shaped to a degree." One morning Thorarin, who, with other trusted ones, slept in Olaf's apartment, was lazily dozing and yawning, and had stretched one of his feet out of the bed before the king awoke. The foot was still there when Olaf did open his bright eyes, which instantly lighted on this foot.

"Well, here is a foot," says Olaf, gayly, "which one seldom sees the match of; I durst venture there is not another so ugly in this city of Nidaros."

"Hah, king!" said Thorarin, "there are few things one cannot match if one seek long and take pains. I would bet, with thy permission, King, to find an uglier."

"Done!" cried Olaf. Upon which Thorarin stretched out the other foot.

"A still uglier," cried he; "for it has lost the little toe."

"Ho, ho!" said Olaf; "but it is I who have gained the bet. The *less* of an ugly thing the less ugly, not the more!"

Loyal Thorarin respectfully submitted.

"What is to be my penalty, then? The king it is that must decide."

"To take me that wicked old Raerik to Leif Ericson in Greenland."

Which the Icelander did; leaving two vacant seats henceforth at Olaf's table. Leif Ericson, son of Eric discoverer of America, quietly managed Raerik henceforth; sent him to Iceland,—I think to father Eric himself; certainly to some safe hand there, in whose house, or in some still quieter neighboring lodging, at his own choice, old Raerik spent the last three years of his life in a perfectly quiescent manner.

Olaf's struggles in the matter of religion had actually settled that question in Norway. By these rough methods of his, whatever we may think of them, Heathenism had got itself smashed dead; and was no more heard of in that country. Olaf himself was evidently a highly devout and pious man;—whosoever is born with Olaf's temper now will still find, as Olaf did, new and infinite field for it! Christianity in Norway had the like fertility as in other countries; or even rose to a higher, and what Dahlmann thinks, exuberant pitch, in the course of the two centuries which followed that of Olaf. Him all testimony represents to us as a most righteous no less than most religious king. Continually vigilant, just, and rigorous was Olaf's administration of the laws; repression of robbery, punishment of injustice, stern repayment of evil–doers, wherever he could lay hold of them.

Among the Bonder or opulent class, and indeed everywhere, for the poor too can be sinners and need punishment, Olaf had, by this course of conduct, naturally made enemies. His severity so visible to all, and the justice and infinite beneficence of it so invisible except to a very few. But, at any rate, his reign for the first ten years was victorious; and might have been so to the end, had it not been intersected, and interfered with, by King Knut in his far bigger orbit and current of affairs and interests. Knut's English affairs and Danish being all settled to his mind, he seems, especially after that year of pilgrimage to Rome, and association with the Pontiffs and Kaisers of the world on that occasion, to have turned his more particular attention upon Norway, and the claims he himself had there. Jarl Hakon, too, sister's son of Knut, and always well seen by him, had long been busy in this direction, much forgetful of that oath to Olaf when his barge got canted over by the cable of two capstans, and his life was given him, not without conditions altogether!

About the year 1026 there arrived two splendid persons out of England, bearing King Knut the Great's letter and seal, with a message, likely enough to be far from welcome to Olaf. For some days Olaf refused to see them or their letter, shrewdly guessing what the purport would be. Which indeed was couched in mild language, but of sharp meaning enough: a notice to King Olaf namely, That Norway was properly, by just heritage, Knut the Great's; and that Olaf must become the great Knut's liegeman, and pay tribute to him, or worse would follow. King Olaf listening to these two splendid persons and their letter, in indignant silence till they quite ended, made answer: "I have heard say, by old accounts there are, that King Gorm of Denmark [Blue-tooth's father, Knut's great-grandfather] was considered but a small king; having Denmark only and few people to rule over. But the kings who succeeded him thought that insufficient for them; and it has since come so far that King Knut rules over both Denmark and England, and has conquered for himself a part of Scotland. And now he claims also my paternal bit of heritage; cannot be contented without that too. Does he wish to rule over all the countries of the North? Can he eat up all the kale in England itself, this Knut the Great? He shall do that, and reduce his England to a desert, before I lay my head in his hands, or show him any other kind of vassalage. And so I bid you tell him these my words: I will defend Norway with battle-axe and sword as long as life is given me, and will pay tax to no man for my kingdom." Words which naturally irritated Knut to a high degree.

Next year accordingly (year 1027), tenth or eleventh year of Olaf's reign, there came bad rumors out of England: That Knut was equipping an immense army,—land-army, and such a fleet as had never sailed before; Knut's own ship in it,—a Gold Dragon with no fewer than sixty benches of oars. Olaf and Onund King of Sweden, whose sister he had married, well guessed whither this armament was bound. They were friends withal, they recognized their common peril in this imminence; and had, in repeated consultations, taken measures the best that their united skill (which I find was mainly Olaf's but loyally accepted by the other) could suggest. It was in this year that Olaf (with his Swedish king assisting) did his grand feat upon Knut in Lymfjord of Jutland, which was already spoken of. The special circumstances of which were these:

Knut's big armament arriving on the Jutish coasts too late in the season, and the coast country lying all plundered into temporary wreck by the two Norse kings, who shrank away on sight of Knut, there was nothing could be done upon them by Knut this year,—or, if anything, what? Knut's ships ran into Lymfjord, the safe-sheltered frith, or intricate long straggle of friths and straits, which almost cuts Jutland in two in that region; and lay safe, idly rocking on the waters there, uncertain what to do farther. At last he steered in his big ship and some others, deeper into the interior of Lymfjord, deeper and deeper onwards to the mouth of a big river called the Helge (Helge-aa, the Holy River, not discoverable in my poor maps, but certainly enough still existing and still flowing somewhere among those intricate straits and friths), towards the bottom of which Helge river lay, in some safe nook, the small combined Swedish and Norse fleet, under the charge of Onund, the Swedish king, while at the top or source, which is a biggish mountain lake, King Olaf had been doing considerable engineering works, well suited to such an occasion, and was now ready at a moment's notice. Knut's fleet having idly taken station here, notice from the Swedish king was instantly sent; instantly Olaf's well−engineered flood−gates were thrown open; from the swollen lake a huge deluge of water was let loose; Olaf himself with all his people hastening down to join his Swedish friend, and get on board in time; Helge river all the while alongside of him, with ever−increasing roar, and wider−spreading deluge, hastening down the steeps in the night−watches. So that, along with Olaf or some way ahead of him, came immeasurable roaring waste of waters upon Knut's negligent fleet; shattered, broke, and stranded many of his ships, and was within a trifle of destroying the Golden Dragon herself, with Knut on board. Olaf and Onund, we need not say, were promptly there in person, doing their very best; the railings of the Golden Dragon, however, were too high for their little ships; and Jarl Ulf, husband of Knut's sister, at the top of his speed, courageously intervening, spoiled their stratagem, and saved Knut from this very dangerous pass.

Knut did nothing more this winter. The two Norse kings, quite unequal to attack such an armament, except by ambush and engineering, sailed away; again plundering at discretion on the Danish coast; carrying into Sweden great booties and many prisoners; but obliged to lie fixed all winter; and indeed to leave their fleets there for a series of winters,—Knut's fleet, posted at Elsinore on both sides of the Sound, rendering all egress from the Baltic impossible, except at his pleasure. Ulf's opportune deliverance of his royal brother−in−law did not much bestead poor Ulf himself. He had been in disfavor before, pardoned with difficulty, by Queen Emma's intercession; an ambitious, officious, pushing, stirring, and, both in England and Denmark, almost dangerous man; and this conspicuous accidental merit only awoke new jealousy in Knut. Knut, finding nothing pass the Sound worth much blockading, went ashore; "and the day before Michaelmas," says Snorro, "rode with a great retinue to Roeskilde." Snorro continues his tragic narrative of what befell there:

"There Knut's brother−in−law, Jarl Ulf, had prepared a great feast for him. The Jarl was the most agreeable of hosts; but the King was silent and sullen. The Jarl talked to him in every way to make him cheerful, and brought forward everything he could think of to amuse him; but the King remained stern, and speaking little. At last the Jarl proposed a game of chess, which he agreed to. A chess−board was produced, and they played together. Jarl Ulf was hasty in temper, stiff, and in nothing yielding; but everything he managed went on well in his hands: and he was a great warrior, about whom there are many stories. He was the most powerful man in Denmark next to the King. Jarl Ulf's sister, Gyda, was married to Jarl Gudin (Godwin) Ulfnadson; and their sons were, Harald King of England, and Jarl Tosti, Jarl Walthiof, Jarl Mauro–Kaare, and Jarl Svein. Gyda was the name of their daughter, who was married to the English King Edward, the Good (whom we call the Confessor).

"When they had played a while, the King made a false move; on which the Jarl took a knight from him; but the King set the piece on the board again, and told the Jarl to make another move. But the Jarl flew angry, tumbled the chess–board over, rose, and went away. The King said, 'Run thy ways, Ulf the Fearful.' The Jarl turned round at the door and said, 'Thou wouldst have run farther at Helge river hadst thou been left to battle there. Thou didst not call me Ulf the Fearful when I hastened to thy help while the Swedes were beating thee like a dog.' The Jarl then went out, and went to bed.

"The following morning, while the King was putting on his clothes, he said to his footboy, 'Go thou to Jarl Ulf and kill him.' The lad went, was away a while, and then came back. The King said, 'Hast thou killed the Jarl?' 'I did not kill him, for he was gone to St. Lucius's church.' There was a man called Ivar the White, a Norwegian by birth, who was the King's courtman and chamberlain. The King said to him, 'Go thou and kill the Jarl.' Ivar went to the church, and in at the choir, and thrust his sword through the Jarl, who died on the spot. Then Ivar went to the King, with the bloody sword in his hand.

"The King said, 'Hast thou killed the Jarl?' 'I have killed him,' said he. 'Thou hast done well,' answered the King." I

From a man who built so many churches (one on each battlefield where he had fought, to say nothing of the others), and who had in him such depths of real devotion and other fine cosmic quality, this does seem rather strong! But it is characteristic, withal,—of the man, and perhaps of the times still more.[14] In any case, it is an event worth noting, the slain Jarl Ulf and his connections being of importance in the history of Denmark and of England also. Ulf's wife was Astrid, sister of Knut, and their only child was Svein, styled afterwards "Svein Estrithson" ("Astrid–son") when he became noted in the world,—at this time a beardless youth, who, on the back of this tragedy, fled hastily to Sweden, where were friends of Ulf. After some ten years' eclipse there, Knut and both his sons being now dead, Svein reappeared in Denmark under a new and eminent figure, "Jarl of Denmark," highest Liegeman to the then sovereign there. Broke his oath to said sovereign, declared himself, Svein Estrithson, to be real King of Denmark; and, after much preliminary trouble, and many beatings and disastrous flights to and fro, became in effect such,—to the wonder of mankind; for he had not had one victory to cheer him on, or any good luck or merit that one sees, except that of surviving longer than some others. Nevertheless he came to be the Restorer, so called, of Danish independence; sole remaining representative of Knut (or Knut's sister), of Fork–beard, Blue–tooth, and Old Gorm; and ancestor of all the subsequent kings of Denmark for some 400 years; himself coming, as we see, only by the Distaff side, all of the Sword or male side having died so soon. Early death, it has been observed, was the Great Knut's allotment, and all his posterity's as well;—fatal limit (had there been no others, which we see there were) to his becoming "Charlemagne of the North" in any considerable degree! Jarl Ulf, as we have seen, had a sister, Gyda by name, wife to Earl Godwin ("Gudin Ulfnadsson," as Snorro calls him) a very memorable Englishman, whose son and hers, King Harald, *Harold* in English books, is the memorablest of all. These things ought to be better known to English antiquaries, and will perhaps be alluded to again.

This pretty little victory or affront, gained over Knut in *Lymfjord*, was among the last successes of Olaf against that mighty man. Olaf, the skilful captain he was, need not have despaired to defend his Norway against Knut and all the world. But he learned henceforth, month by month ever more tragically, that his own people, seeing softer prospects under Knut, and in particular the chiefs of them, industriously bribed by Knut for years past, had fallen away from him; and that his means of defence were gone. Next summer, Knut's grand fleet sailed, unopposed, along the coast of Norway; Knut summoning a Thing every here and there, and in all of them meeting nothing but sky–high acclamation and acceptance. Olaf, with some twelve little ships, all he now had, lay quiet in some safe fjord, near Lindenaes, what we now call the Naze, behind some little solitary isles on the southeast of Norway there; till triumphant Knut had streamed home again. Home to England again "Sovereign of Norway" now, with nephew Hakon appointed Jarl and Vice–regent under him! This was the news Olaf met on venturing out; and that his worst anticipations were not beyond the sad truth all, or almost all, the chief Bonders and men of weight in Norway had declared against him, and stood with triumphant Knut.

Olaf, with his twelve poor ships, steered vigorously along the coast to collect money and force,—if such could now anywhere be had. He himself was resolute to hold out, and try. "Sailing swiftly with a fair wind, morning cloudy with some showers," he passed the coast of Jedderen, which was Erling Skjalgson's country, when he got sure notice of an endless multitude of ships, war–ships, armed merchant ships, all kinds of shipping–craft, down to fishermen's boats, just getting under way against him, under the command of Erling Skjalgson,— the powerfulest of his subjects, once much a friend of Olaf's but now gone against him to this length, thanks to Olaf's severity of justice, and Knut's abundance in gold and promises for years back. To that complexion had it come with Erling; sailing with this immense assemblage of the naval people and populace of Norway to seize King Olaf, and bring him to the great Knut dead or alive.

Erling had a grand new ship of his own, which far outsailed the general miscellany of rebel ships, and was visibly fast gaining distance on Olaf himself,—who well understood what Erling's puzzle was, between the tail of his game (the miscellany of rebel ships, namely) that could not come up, and the head or general prize of the game which was crowding all sail to get away; and Olaf took advantage of the same. "Lower your sails!" said Olaf to his men (though we must go slower).

"Ho you, we have lost sight of them!" said Erling to his, and put on all his speed; Olaf going, soon after this, altogether invisible,—behind a little island that he knew of, whence into a certain fjord or bay (Bay of Fungen on the maps), which he thought would suit him. "Halt here, and get out your arms," said Olaf, and had not to wait long till Erling came bounding in, past the rocky promontory, and with astonishment beheld Olaf's fleet of twelve with their battle–axes and their grappling–irons all in perfect readiness. These fell on him, the unready Erling, simultaneous, like a cluster of angry bees; and in a few minutes cleared his ship of men altogether, except Erling himself. Nobody asked his life, nor probably would have got it if he had. Only Erling still stood erect on a high place on the poop, fiercely defensive, and very difficult to get at. "Could not be reached at all," says Snorro, "except by spears or arrows, and these he warded off with untiring dexterity; no man in Norway, it was said, had ever defended himself so long alone against many,"—an almost invincible Erling, had his cause been good. Olaf himself noticed Erling's behavior, and said to him, from the foredeck below, "Thou hast turned against me to–day, Erling." "The eagles fight breast to breast," answers he. This was a speech of the king's to Erling once long ago, while they stood fighting, not as now, but side by side. The king, with some transient thought of possibility going through his head, rejoins, "Wilt thou surrender, Erling?" "That will I," answered he; took the helmet off his head; laid down sword and shield; and went forward to the forecastle deck. The king pricked, I think not very harshly, into Erling's chin or beard with the point of his battle–axe, saying, "I must mark thee as traitor to thy Sovereign, though." Whereupon one of the bystanders,

Aslak Fitiaskalle, stupidly and fiercely burst up; smote Erling on the head with his axe; so that it struck fast in his brain and was instantly the death of Erling. "Ill–luck attend thee for that stroke; thou hast struck Norway out of my hand by it!" cried the king to Aslak; but forgave the poor fellow, who had done it meaning well. The insurrectionary Bonder fleet arriving soon after, as if for certain victory, was struck with astonishment at this Erling catastrophe; and being now without any leader of authority, made not the least attempt at battle; but, full of discouragement and consternation, thankfully allowed Olaf to sail away on his northward voyage, at discretion; and themselves went off lamenting, with Erling's dead body.

This small victory was the last that Olaf had over his many enemies at present. He sailed along, still northward, day after day; several important people joined him; but the news from landward grew daily more ominous: Bonders busily arming to rear of him; and ahead, Hakon still more busily at Trondhjem, now near by, "—and he will end thy days, King, if he have strength enough!" Olaf paused; sent scouts to a hill–top: "Hakon's armament visible enough, and under way hitherward, about the Isle of Bjarno, yonder!" Soon after, Olaf himself saw the Bonder armament of twenty–five ships, from the southward, sail past in the distance to join that of Hakon; and, worse still, his own ships, one and another (seven in all), were slipping off on a like errand! He made for the Fjord of Fodrar, mouth of the rugged strath called Valdal,—which I think still knows Olaf and has now an "Olaf's Highway," where, nine centuries ago, it scarcely had a path. Olaf entered this fjord, had his land–tent set up, and a cross beside it, on the small level green behind the promontory there. Finding that his twelve poor ships were now reduced to five, against a world all risen upon him, he could not but see and admit to himself that there was no chance left; and that he must withdraw across the mountains and wait for a better time.

His journey through that wild country, in these forlorn and straitened circumstances, has a mournful dignity and homely pathos, as described by Snorro: how he drew up his five poor ships upon the beach, packed all their furniture away, and with his hundred or so of attendants and their journey–baggage, under guidance of some friendly Bonder, rode up into the desert and foot of the mountains; scaled, after three days' effort (as if by miracle, thought his attendants and thought Snorro), the well–nigh precipitous slope that led across, never without miraculous aid from Heaven and Olaf could baggage–wagons have ascended that path! In short, How he fared along, beset by difficulties and the mournfulest thoughts; but patiently persisted, steadfastly trusted in God; and was fixed to return, and by God's help try again. An evidently very pious and devout man; a good man struggling with adversity, such as the gods, we may still imagine with the ancients, do look down upon as their noblest sight.

He got to Sweden, to the court of his brother–in–law; kindly and nobly enough received there, though gradually, perhaps, ill–seen by the now authorities of Norway. So that, before long, he quitted Sweden; left his queen there with her only daughter, his and hers, the only child they had; he himself had an only son, "by a bondwoman," Magnus by name, who came to great things afterwards; of whom, and of which, by and by. With this bright little boy, and a selected escort of attendants, he moved away to Russia, to King Jarroslav; where he might wait secure against all risk of hurting kind friends by his presence. He seems to have been an exile altogether some two years,—such is one's vague notion; for there is no chronology in Snorro or his Sagas, and one is reduced to guessing and inferring. He had reigned over Norway, reckoning from the first days of his landing there to those last of his leaving it across the Dovrefjeld, about fifteen years, ten of them shiningly victorious.

The news from Norway were naturally agitating to King Olaf and, in the fluctuation of events there, his purposes and prospects varied much. He sometimes thought of pilgriming to Jerusalem, and a henceforth exclusively religious life; but for most part his pious thoughts themselves gravitated towards Norway, and a stroke for his old place and task there, which he steadily considered to have been committed to him by God. Norway, by the rumors, was evidently not at rest. Jarl Hakon, under the high patronage of his uncle, had lasted there but a little while. I know not that his government was especially unpopular, nor whether he himself much remembered his broken oath. It appears, however, he had left in England a beautiful bride; and considering farther that in England only could bridal ornaments and other wedding outfit of a sufficiently royal kind be found, he set sail thither, to fetch her and them himself. One evening of wildish–looking weather he was seen about the northeast corner of the Pentland Frith; the night rose to be tempestuous; Hakon or any timber of his fleet was never seen more. Had all gone down,—broken oaths, bridal hopes, and all else; mouse and man,—into the roaring waters. There was no farther Opposition–line; the like of which had lasted ever since old heathen Hakon Jarl, down to this his grandson Hakon's finis in the Pentland Frith. With this Hakon's disappearance it now disappeared.

Indeed Knut himself, though of an empire suddenly so great, was but a temporary phenomenon. Fate had decided that the grand and wise Knut was to be short–lived; and to leave nothing as successors but an ineffectual young Harald Harefoot, who soon perished, and a still stupider fiercely–drinking Harda–Knut, who rushed down of apoplexy (here in London City, as I guess), with the goblet at his mouth, drinking health and happiness at a wedding–feast, also before long.

Hakon having vanished in this dark way, there ensued a pause, both on Knut's part and on Norway's. Pause or interregnum of some months, till it became certain, first, whether Hakon were actually dead, secondly, till Norway, and especially till King Knut himself, could decide what to do. Knut, to the deep disappointment, which had to keep itself silent, of three or four chief Norway men, named none of these three or four Jarl of Norway; but bethought him of a certain Svein, a bastard son of his own,—who, and almost still more his English mother, much desired a career in the world fitter for him, thought they indignantly, than that of captain over Jomsburg, where alone the father had been able to provide for him hitherto. Svein was sent to Norway as king or vice–king for Father Knut; and along with him his fond and vehement mother. Neither of whom gained any favor from the Norse people by the kind of management they ultimately came to show.

Olaf on news of this change, and such uncertainty prevailing everywhere in Norway as to the future course of things, whether Svein would come, as was rumored of at last, and be able to maintain himself if he did,—thought there might be something in it of a chance for himself and his rights. And, after lengthened hesitation, much prayer, pious invocation, and consideration, decided to go and try it. The final grain that had turned the balance, it appears, was a half–waking morning dream, or almost ocular vision he had of his glorious cousin Olaf Tryggveson, who severely admonished, exhorted, and encouraged him; and disappeared grandly, just in the instant of Olaf's awakening; so that Olaf almost fancied he had seen the very figure of him, as it melted into air. "Let us on, let us on!" thought Olaf always after that. He left his son, not in Russia, but in Sweden with the Queen, who proved very good and carefully helpful in wise ways to him:—in Russia Olaf had now nothing more to do but give his grateful adieus, and get ready.

His march towards Sweden, and from that towards Norway and the passes of the mountains, down Vaerdal, towards Stickelstad, and the crisis that awaited, is beautifully depicted by Snorro. It has, all of it, the description (and we see clearly, the fact itself had), a kind of pathetic grandeur, simplicity, and rude nobleness; something Epic or Homeric, without the metre or the singing of Homer, but with all the sincerity, rugged truth to nature, and much more of piety, devoutness, reverence for what is forever High in this Universe, than meets us in those old Greek Ballad–mongers. Singularly visual all of it, too, brought home in every particular to one's imagination, so that it stands out almost as a thing one actually saw.

Olaf had about three thousand men with him; gathered mostly as he fared along through Norway. Four hundred, raised by one Dag, a kinsman whom he had found in Sweden and persuaded to come with him, marched usually in a separate body; and were, or might have been, rather an important element. Learning that the Bonders were all arming, especially in Trondhjem country, Olaf streamed down towards them in the closest order he could. By no means very close, subsistence even for three thousand being difficult in such a country. His speech was almost always free and cheerful, though his thoughts always naturally were of a high and earnest, almost sacred tone; devout above all. Stickelstad, a small poor hamlet still standing where the valley ends, was seen by Olaf, and tacitly by the Bonders as well, to be the natural place for offering battle. There Olaf issued out from the hills one morning: drew himself up according to the best rules of Norse tactics, rules of little complexity, but perspicuously true to the facts. I think he had a clear open ground still rather raised above the plain in front; he could see how the Bonder army had not yet quite arrived, but was pouring forward, in spontaneous rows or groups, copiously by every path. This was thought to be the biggest army that ever met in Norway; "certainly not much fewer than a hundred times a hundred men," according to Snorro; great Bonders several of them, small Bonders very many,—all of willing mind, animated with a hot sense of intolerable injuries. "King Olaf had punished great and small with equal rigor," says Snorro; "which appeared to the chief people of the country too severe; and animosity rose to the highest when they lost relatives by the King's just sentence, although they were in reality guilty. He again would rather renounce his dignity than omit righteous judgment. The accusation against him, of being stingy with his money, was not just, for he was a most generous man towards his friends. But that alone was the cause of the discontent raised against him, that he appeared hard and severe in his retributions. Besides, King Knut offered large sums of money, and the great chiefs were corrupted by this, and by his offering them greater dignities than they had possessed before." On these grounds, against the intolerable man, great and small were now pouring along by every path.

Olaf perceived it would still be some time before the Bonder army was in rank. His own Dag of Sweden, too, was not yet come up; he was to have the right banner; King Olaf's own being the middle or grand one; some other person the third or left banner. All which being perfectly ranked and settled, according to the best rules, and waiting only the arrival of Dag, Olaf bade his men sit down, and freshen themselves with a little rest. There were religious services gone through: a matins–worship such as there have been few; sternly earnest to the heart of it, and deep as death and eternity, at least on Olaf's own part. For the rest Thormod sang a stave of the fiercest Skaldic poetry that was in him; all the army straightway sang it in chorus with fiery mind. The Bonder of the nearest farm came up, to tell Olaf that he also wished to fight for him "Thanks to thee; but don't," said Olaf; "stay at home rather, that the wounded may have some shelter." To this Bonder, Olaf delivered all the money he had, with solemn order to lay out the whole of it in masses and prayers for the souls of such of his enemies as fell. "Such of thy enemies, King?" "Yes, surely," said Olaf, "my friends will all either conquer, or go whither I also am going."

At last the Bonder army too was got ranked; three commanders, one of them with a kind of loose chief command, having settled to take charge of it; and began to shake itself towards actual advance. Olaf, in the mean while, had laid his head on the knees of Finn Arneson, his trustiest man, and fallen fast asleep. Finn's brother, Kalf Arneson, once a warm friend of Olaf, was chief of the three commanders on the opposite side. Finn and he addressed angry speech to one another from the opposite ranks, when they came near enough. Finn, seeing the enemy fairly approach, stirred Olaf from his sleep. "Oh, why hast thou wakened me from such a dream?" said Olaf, in a deeply solemn tone. "What dream was it, then?" asked Finn. "I dreamt that there rose a ladder here reaching up to very Heaven," said Olaf; "I had climbed and climbed, and got to the very last step, and should have entered there hadst thou given me another moment." "King, I doubt thou art *fey*; I do not quite like that dream."

The actual fight began about one of the clock in a most bright last day of July, and was very fierce and hot, especially on the part of Olaf's men, who shook the others back a little, though fierce enough they too; and had Dag been on the ground, which he wasn't yet, it was thought victory might have been won. Soon after battle joined, the sky grew of a ghastly brass or copper color, darker and darker, till thick night involved all things; and did not clear away again till battle was near ending. Dag, with his four hundred, arrived in the darkness, and made a furious charge, what was afterwards, in the speech of the people, called "Dag's storm." Which had nearly prevailed, but could not quite; victory again inclining to the so vastly larger party. It is uncertain still how the matter would have gone; for Olaf himself was now fighting with his own hand, and doing deadly execution on his busiest enemies to right and to left. But one of these chief rebels, Thorer Hund (thought to have learnt magic from the Laplanders, whom he long traded with, and made money by), mysteriously would not fall for Olaf's best strokes. Best strokes brought only dust from the (enchanted) deer−skin coat of the fellow, to Olaf's surprise,—when another of the rebel chiefs rushed forward, struck Olaf with his battle−axe, a wild slashing wound, and miserably broke his thigh, so that he staggered or was supported back to the nearest stone; and there sat down, lamentably calling on God to help him in this bad hour. Another rebel of note (the name of him long memorable in Norway) slashed or stabbed Olaf a second time, as did then a third. Upon which the noble Olaf sank dead; and forever quitted this doghole of a world,—little worthy of such men as Olaf one sometimes thinks. But that too is a mistake, and even an important one, should we persist in it.

With Olaf's death the sky cleared again. Battle, now near done, ended with complete victory to the rebels, and next to no pursuit or result, except the death of Olaf everybody hastening home, as soon as the big Duel had decided itself. Olaf's body was secretly carried, after dark, to some out−house on the farm near the spot; whither a poor blind beggar, creeping in for shelter that very evening, was miraculously restored to sight. And, truly with a notable, almost miraculous, speed, the feelings of all Norway for King Olaf changed themselves, and were turned upside down, "within a year," or almost within a day. Superlative example of *Extinctus amabitur idem.* Not "Olaf the Thick−set" any longer, but "Olaf the Blessed" or Saint, now clearly in Heaven; such the name and character of him from that time to this. Two churches dedicated to him (out of four that once stood) stand in London at this moment. And the miracles that have been done there, not to speak of Norway and Christendom elsewhere, in his name, were numerous and great for long centuries afterwards. Visibly a Saint Olaf ever since; and, indeed, in *Bollandus* or elsewhere, I have seldom met with better stuff to make a Saint of, or a true World−Hero in all good senses.

Speaking of the London Olaf Churches, I should have added that from one of these the thrice−famous Tooley Street gets its name,—where those Three Tailors, addressing Parliament and the Universe, sublimely styled themselves, "We, the People of England." Saint Olave Street, Saint Oley Street, Stooley Street, Tooley Street; such are the metamorphoses of human fame in the world!

The battle–day of Stickelstad, King Olaf's death–day, is generally believed to have been Wednesday, July 31, 1033. But on investigation, it turns out that there was no total eclipse of the sun visible in Norway that year; though three years before, there was one; but on the 29th instead of the 31st. So that the exact date still remains uncertain; Dahlmann, the latest critic, inclining for 1030, and its indisputable eclipse.[15]

CHAPTER XI. MAGNUS THE GOOD AND OTHERS.

St. Olaf is the highest of these Norway Kings, and is the last that much attracts us. For this reason, if a reason were not superfluous, we might here end our poor reminiscences of those dim Sovereigns. But we will, nevertheless, for the sake of their connection with bits of English History, still hastily mention the Dames of one or two who follow, and who throw a momentary gleam of life and illumination on events and epochs that have fallen so extinct among ourselves at present, though once they were so momentous and memorable.

The new King Svein from Jomsburg, Knut's natural son, had no success in Norway, nor seems to have deserved any. His English mother and he were found to be grasping, oppressive persons; and awoke, almost from the instant that Olaf was suppressed and crushed away from Norway into Heaven, universal odium more and more in that country. Well–deservedly, as still appears; for their taxings and extortions of malt, of herring, of meal, smithwork and every article taxable in Norway, were extreme; and their service to the country otherwise nearly imperceptible. In brief their one basis there was the power of Knut the Great; and that, like all earthly things, was liable to sudden collapse,—and it suffered such in a notable degree. King Knut, hardly yet of middle age, and the greatest King in the then world, died at Shaftesbury, in 1035, as Dahlmann thinks[16],—leaving two legitimate sons and a busy, intriguing widow (Norman Emma, widow of Ethelred the Unready), mother of the younger of these two; neither of whom proved to have any talent or any continuance. In spite of Emma's utmost efforts, Harald, the elder son of Knut, not hers, got England for his kingdom; Emma and her Harda–Knut had to be content with Denmark, and go thither, much against their will. Harald in England,—light–going little figure like his father before him,—got the name of Harefoot here; and might have done good work among his now orderly and settled people; but he died almost within year and day; and has left no trace among us, except that of "Harefoot," from his swift mode of walking. Emma and her Harda–Knut now returned joyful to England. But the violent, idle, and drunken Harda–Knut did no good there; and, happily for England and him, soon suddenly ended, by stroke of apoplexy at a marriage festival, as mentioned above. In Denmark he had done still less good. And indeed,—under him, in a year or two, the grand imperial edifice, laboriously built by Knut's valor and wisdom, had already tumbled all to the ground, in a most unexpected and remarkable way. As we are now to indicate with all brevity.

Svein's tyrannies in Norway had wrought such fruit that, within the four years after Olaf's death, the chief men in Norway, the very slayers of King Olaf, Kalf Arneson at the head of them, met secretly once or twice; and unanimously agreed that Kalf Arneson must go to Sweden, or to Russia itself; seek young Magnus, son of Olaf home: excellent Magnus, to be king over all Norway and them, instead of this intolerable Svein. Which was at once done,—Magnus brought home in a kind of triumph, all Norway waiting for him. Intolerable Svein had already been rebelled against: some years before this, a certain young Tryggve out of Ireland, authentic son of Olaf Tryggveson, and of that fine Irish Princess who chose him in his low habiliments and low estate, and took him over to her own Green Island,—this royal young Tryggve Olafson had invaded the usurper Svein, in a fierce, valiant, and determined manner; and though with too small a party, showed excellent fight for some time; till Svein, zealously bestirring himself, managed to get him beaten and killed. But that was a couple of years ago; the party still too small, not including one and all as now! Svein, without stroke of sword this time, moved off towards Denmark; never showing face in Norway again. His drunken brother, Harda–Knut, received him brother–like; even gave him some territory to rule over and subsist upon. But he lived only a short while; was gone before Harda–Knut himself; and we will mention him no more.

Magnus was a fine bright young fellow, and proved a valiant, wise, and successful King, known among his people as Magnus the Good. He was only natural son of King Olaf but that made little difference in those times and there. His strange–looking, unexpected Latin name he got in this way: Alfhild, his mother, a slave through ill–luck of war, though nobly born, was seen to be in a hopeful way; and it was known in the King's house how intimately Olaf was connected with that occurrence, and how much he loved this "King's serving–maid," as she was commonly designated. Alfhild was brought to bed late at night; and all the world, especially King Olaf was asleep; Olaf's strict rule, then and always, being, Don't awaken me:—seemingly a man sensitive about his sleep. The child was a boy, of rather weakly aspect; no important person present, except Sigvat, the King's Icelandic Skald, who happened to be still awake; and the Bishop of Norway, who, I suppose, had been sent for in hurry. "What is to be done?" said the Bishop: "here is an infant in pressing need of baptism; and we know not what the name is: go, Sigvat, awaken the King, and ask." "I dare not for my life," answered Sigvat; "King's orders are rigorous on that point." "But if the child die unbaptized," said the Bishop, shuddering; too certain, he and everybody, where the child would go in that case! "I will myself give him a name," said Sigvat, with a desperate concentration of all his faculties; "he shall be namesake of the greatest of mankind,—imperial Carolus Magnus; let us call the infant Magnus!" King Olaf, on the morrow, asked rather sharply how Sigvat had dared take such a liberty; but excused Sigvat, seeing what the perilous alternative was. And Magnus, by such accident, this boy was called; and he, not another, is the prime origin and introducer of that name Magnus, which occurs rather frequently, not among the Norman Kings only, but by and by among the Danish and Swedish; and, among the Scandinavian populations, appears to be rather frequent to this day.

Magnus, a youth of great spirit, whose own, and standing at his beck, all Norway now was, immediately smote home on Denmark; desirous naturally of vengeance for what it had done to Norway, and the sacred kindred of Magnus. Denmark, its great Knut gone, and nothing but a drunken Harda–Knut, fugitive Svein and Co., there in his stead, was become a weak dislocated Country. And Magnus plundered in it, burnt it, beat it, as often as he pleased; Harda–Knut struggling what he could to make resistance or reprisals, but never once getting any victory over Magnus. Magnus, I perceive, was, like his Father, a skilful as well as valiant fighter by sea and land; Magnus, with good battalions, and probably backed by immediate alliance with Heaven and St. Olaf, as was then the general belief or surmise about him, could not easily be beaten. And the truth is, he never was, by Harda–Knut or any other. Harda–Knut's last transaction with him was, To make a firm Peace and even Family–treaty sanctioned by all the grandees of both countries, who did indeed mainly themselves make it; their two Kings assenting: That there should be perpetual Peace, and no thought of war more, between Denmark and Norway; and that, if either of the Kings died childless while the other was reigning, the other should succeed him in both Kingdoms. A magnificent arrangement, such as has several times been made in the world's history; but which in this instance, what is very singular, took actual effect; drunken Harda– Knut dying so speedily, and Magnus being the man he was. One would like to give the date of this remarkable Treaty; but cannot with precision. Guess somewhere about 1040:[17] actual fruition of it came to Magnus, beyond question, in 1042, when Harda–Knut drank that wassail bowl at the wedding in Lambeth, and fell down dead; which in the Saxon Chronicle is dated 3d June of that year. Magnus at once went to Denmark on hearing this event; was joyfully received by the headmen there, who indeed, with their fellows in Norway, had been main contrivers of the Treaty; both Countries longing for mutual peace, and the end of such incessant broils.

Magnus was triumphantly received as King in Denmark. The only unfortunate thing was, that Svein Estrithson, the exile son of Ulf, Knut's Brother–in–law, whom Knut, as we saw, had summarily killed twelve years before, emerged from his exile in Sweden in a flattering form; and proposed that Magnus should make him Jarl of Denmark, and general administrator there, in his own stead. To which the sanguine Magnus, in spite of advice to the contrary, insisted on acceding. "Too powerful a Jarl," said Einar Tamberskelver—the same Einar whose bow was heard to break in Olaf Tryggveson's last battle ("Norway breaking from thy hand, King!"), who had now become Magnus's chief man, and had long been among the highest chiefs in Norway; "too powerful a Jarl," said Einar earnestly. But Magnus disregarded it; and a troublesome experience had to teach him that it was true. In about a year, crafty Svein, bringing ends to meet, got himself declared King of Denmark for his own behoof, instead of Jarl for another's: and had to be beaten and driven out by Magnus. Beaten every year; but almost always returned next year, for a new beating,—almost, though not altogether; having at length got one dreadful smashing–down and half–killing, which held him quiet for a while,—so long as Magnus lived. Nay in the end, he made good his point, as if by mere patience in being beaten; and did become King himself, and progenitor of all the Kings that followed. King Svein Estrithson; so called from Astrid or Estrith, his mother, the great Knut's sister, daughter of Svein Forkbeard by that amazing Sigrid the Proud, who *burnt* those two ineligible suitors of hers both at once, and got a switch on the face from Olaf Tryggveson, which proved the death of that high man.

But all this fine fortune of the often beaten Estrithson was posterior to Magnus's death; who never would have suffered it, had he been alive. Magnus was a mighty fighter; a fiery man; very proud and positive, among other qualities, and had such luck as was never seen before. Luck invariably good, said everybody; never once was beaten,—which proves, continued everybody, that his Father Olaf and the miraculous power of Heaven were with him always. Magnus, I believe, did put down a great deal of anarchy in those countries. One of his earliest enterprises was to abolish Jomsburg, and trample out that nest of pirates. Which he managed so completely that Jomsburg remained a mere reminiscence thenceforth; and its place is not now known to any mortal.

One perverse thing did at last turn up in the course of Magnus: a new Claimant for the Crown of Norway, and he a formidable person withal. This was Harald, half–brother of the late Saint Olaf; uncle or half–uncle, therefore, of Magnus himself. Indisputable son of the Saint's mother by St. Olaf's stepfather, who was, himself descended straight from Harald Haarfagr. This new Harald was already much heard of in the world. As an ardent Boy of fifteen he had fought at King Olaf's side at Stickelstad; would not be admonished by the Saint to go away. Got smitten down there, not killed; was smuggled away that night from the field by friendly help; got cured of his wounds, forwarded to Russia, where he grew to man's estate, under bright auspices and successes. Fell in love with the Russian Princess, but could not get her to wife; went off thereupon to Constantinople as Vaeringer (Life–Guardsman of the Greek Kaiser); became Chief Captain of the Vaeringers, invincible champion of the poor Kaisers that then were, and filled all the East with the shine and noise of his exploits. An authentic *Waring* or *Baring*, such the surname we now have derived from these people; who were an important institution in those Greek countries for several ages: Vaeringer Life–Guard, consisting of Norsemen, with sometimes a few English among them. Harald had innumerable adventures, nearly always successful, sing the Skalds; gained a great deal of wealth, gold ornaments, and gold coin; had even Queen Zoe (so they sing, though falsely) enamored of him at one time; and was himself a Skald of eminence; some of whose verses, by no means the worst of their kind, remain to this day.

This character of Waring much distinguishes Harald to me; the only Vaeringer of whom I could ever get the least biography, true or half–true. It seems the Greek History–books but indifferently correspond with these Saga records; and scholars say there could have been no considerable romance between Zoe and him, Zoe at that date being 60 years of age! Harald's own lays say nothing of any Zoe, but are still full of longing for his Russian Princess far away.

At last, what with Zoes, what with Greek perversities and perfidies, and troubles that could not fail, he determined on quitting Greece; packed up his immensities of wealth in succinct shape, and actually returned to Russia, where new honors and favors awaited him from old friends, and especially, if I mistake not, the hand of that adorable Princess, crown of all his wishes for the time being. Before long, however, he decided farther to look after his Norway Royal heritages; and, for that purpose, sailed in force to the Jarl or quasi–King of Denmark, the often–beaten Svein, who was now in Sweden on his usual winter exile after beating. Svein and he had evidently interests in common. Svein was charmed to see him, so warlike, glorious and renowned a man, with masses of money about him, too. Svein did by and by become treacherous; and even attempted, one night, to assassinate Harald in his bed on board ship: but Harald, vigilant of Svein, and a man of quick and sure insight, had providently gone to sleep elsewhere, leaving a log instead of himself among the blankets. In which log, next morning, treacherous Svein's battle–axe was found deeply sticking: and could not be removed without difficulty! But this was after Harald and King Magnus himself bad begun treating; with the fairest prospects,—which this of the $vein battle–axe naturally tended to forward, as it altogether ended the other copartnery.

Magnus, on first hearing of Vaeringer Harald and his intentions, made instant equipment, and determination to fight his uttermost against the same. But wise persons of influence round him, as did the like sort round Vaeringer Harald, earnestly advised compromise and peaceable agreement. Which, soon after that of Svein's nocturnal battle–axe, was the course adopted; and, to the joy of all parties, did prove a successful solution. Magnus agreed to part his kingdom with Uncle Harald; uncle parting his treasures, or uniting them with Magnus's poverty. Each was to be an independent king, but they were to govern in common; Magnus rather presiding. He, to sit, for example, in the High Seat alone; King Harald opposite him in a seat not quite so high, though if a stranger King came on a visit, both the Norse Kings were to sit in the High Seat. With various other punctilious regulations; which the fiery Magnus was extremely strict with; rendering the mutual relation a very dangerous one, had not both the Kings been honest men, and Harald a much more prudent and tolerant one than Magnus. They, on the whole, never had any weighty quarrel, thanks now and then rather to Harald than to Magnus. Magnus too was very noble; and Harald, with his wide experience and greater length of years, carefully held his heat of temper well covered in.

Prior to Uncle Harald's coming, Magnus had distinguished himself as a Lawgiver. His Code of Laws for the Trondhjem Province was considered a pretty piece of legislation; and in subsequent times got the name of Gray–goose (Gragas); one of the wonderfulest names ever given to a wise Book. Some say it came from the gray color of the parchment, some give other incredible origins; the last guess I have heard is, that the name merely denotes antiquity; the witty name in Norway for a man growing old having been, in those times, that he was now "becoming a gray–goose." Very fantastic indeed; certain, however, that Gray–goose is the name of that venerable Law Book; nay, there is another, still more famous, belonging to Iceland, and not far from a century younger, the Iceland *Gray–goose*. The Norway one is perhaps of date about 1037, the other of about 1118; peace be with them both! Or, if anybody is inclined to such matters let him go to Dahlmann, for the amplest information and such minuteness of detail as might almost enable him to be an Advocate, with Silk Gown, in any Court depending on these Gray–geese.

Magnus did not live long. He had a dream one night of his Father Olaf's coming to him in shining presence, and announcing, That a magnificent fortune and world–great renown was now possible for him; but that perhaps it was his duty to refuse it; in which case his earthly life would be short. "Which way wilt thou do, then?" said the shining presence. "Thou shalt decide for me, Father, thou, not I!" and told his Uncle Harald on the morrow, adding that he thought he should now soon die; which proved to be the fact. The magnificent fortune, so questionable otherwise, has reference, no doubt, to the Conquest of England; to which country Magnus, as rightful and actual King of *Denmark*, as well as undisputed heir to drunken Harda–Knut, by treaty long ago, had now some evident claim. The enterprise itself was reserved to the patient, gay, and prudent Uncle Harald; and to him it did prove fatal,—and merely paved the way for Another, luckier, not likelier!

Svein Estrithson, always beaten during Magnus's life, by and by got an agreement from the prudent Harald to *be* King of Denmark, then; and end these wearisome and ineffectual brabbles; Harald having other work to do. But in the autumn of 1066, Tosti, a younger son of our English Earl Godwin, came to Svein's court with a most important announcement; namely, that King Edward the Confessor, so called, was dead, and that Harold, as the English write it, his eldest brother would give him, Tosti, no sufficient share in the kingship. Which state of matters, if Svein would go ahead with him to rectify it, would be greatly to the advantage of Svein. Svein, taught by many beatings, was too wise for this proposal; refused Tosti, who indignantly stepped over into Norway, and proposed it to King Harald there. Svein really had acquired considerable teaching, I should guess, from his much beating and hard experience in the world; one finds him afterwards the esteemed friend of the famous Historian Adam of Bremen, who reports various wise humanities, and pleasant discoursings with Svein Estrithson.

Early Kings of Norway

As for Harald Hardrade, "Harald the Hard or Severe," as he was now called, Tosti's proposal awakened in him all his old Vaeringer ambitious and cupidities into blazing vehemence. He zealously consented; and at once, with his whole strength, embarked in the adventure. Fitted out two hundred ships, and the biggest army he could carry in them; and sailed with Tosti towards the dangerous Promised Land. Got into the Tyne and took booty; got into the Humber, thence into the Ouse; easily subdued any opposition the official people or their populations could make; victoriously scattered these, victoriously took the City of York in a day; and even got himself homaged there, "King of Northumberland," as per covenant,—Tosti proving honorable,—Tosti and he going with faithful strict copartnery, and all things looking prosperous and glorious. Except only (an important exception!) that they learnt for certain, English Harold was advancing with all his strength; and, in a measurable space of hours, unless care were taken, would be in York himself. Harald and Tosti hastened off to seize the post of Stamford Bridge on Derwent River, six or seven miles east of York City, and there bar this dangerous advent. Their own ships lay not far off in Ouse River, in case of the worst. The battle that ensued the next day, September 20, 1066, is forever memorable in English history.

Snorro gives vividly enough his view of it from the Icelandic side: A ring of stalwart Norsemen, close ranked, with their steel tools in hand; English Harold's Army, mostly cavalry, prancing and pricking all around; trying to find or make some opening in that ring. For a long time trying in vain, till at length, getting them enticed to burst out somewhere in pursuit, they quickly turned round, and quickly made an end, of that matter. Snorro represents English Harold, with a first party of these horse coming up, and, with preliminary salutations, asking if Tosti were there, and if Harald were; making generous proposals to Tosti; but, in regard to Harald and what share of England was to be his, answering Tosti with the words, "Seven feet of English earth, or more if he require it, for a grave." Upon which Tosti, like an honorable man and copartner, said, "No, never; let us fight you rather till we all die." "Who is this that spoke to you?" inquired Harald, when the cavaliers had withdrawn. "My brother Harold," answers Tosti; which looks rather like a Saga, but may be historical after all. Snorro's history of the battle is intelligible only after you have premised to it, what he never hints at, that the scene was on the east side of the bridge and of the Derwent; the great struggle for the bridge, one at last finds, was after the fall of Harald; and to the English Chroniclers, said struggle, which was abundantly severe, is all they know of the battle.

Enraged at that breaking loose of his steel ring of infantry, Norse Harald blazed up into true Norse fury, all the old Vaeringer and Berserkir rage awakening in him; sprang forth into the front of the fight, and mauled and cut and smashed down, on both hands of him, everything he met, irresistible by any horse or man, till an arrow cut him through the windpipe, and laid him low forever. That was the end of King Harald and of his workings in this world. The circumstance that he was a Waring or Baring and had smitten to pieces so many Oriental cohorts or crowds, and had made love–verses (kind of iron madrigals) to his Russian Princess, and caught the fancy of questionable Greek queens, and had amassed such heaps of money, while poor nephew Magnus had only one gold ring (which had been his father's, and even his father's *mother's*, as Uncle Harald noticed), and nothing more whatever of that precious metal to combine with Harald's treasures:—all this is new to me, naturally no hint of it in any English book; and lends some gleam of romantic splendor to that dim business of Stamford Bridge, now fallen so dull and torpid to most English minds, transcendently important as it once was to all Englishmen. Adam of Bremen says, the English got as much gold plunder from Harald's people as was a heavy burden for twelve men;[18] a thing evidently impossible, which nobody need try to believe. Young Olaf, Harald's son, age about sixteen, steering down the Ouse at the top of his speed, escaped home to Norway with all his ships, and subsequently reigned there with Magnus, his brother. Harald's body did lie in English earth for about a year; but was then brought to Norway for burial. He needed more than seven feet of grave, say some; Laing, interpreting Snorro's measurements, makes Harald eight feet in stature,—I do hope, with some error in excess!

CHAPTER XII. OLAF THE TRANQUIL, MAGNUS BAREFOOT, AND SIGURD THE CRUSADER.

The new King Olaf, his brother Magnus having soon died, bore rule in Norway for some five–and–twenty years. Rule soft and gentle, not like his father's, and inclining rather to improvement in the arts and elegancies than to anything severe or dangerously laborious. A slim–built, witty–talking, popular and pretty man, with uncommonly bright eyes, and hair like floss silk: they called him Olaf *Kyrre* (the Tranquil or Easygoing).

The ceremonials of the palace were much improved by him. Palace still continued to be built of huge logs pyramidally sloping upwards, with fireplace in the middle of the floor, and no egress for smoke or ingress for light except right overhead, which, in bad weather, you could shut, or all but shut, with a lid. Lid originally made of mere opaque board, but changed latterly into a light frame, covered (glazed, so to speak) with entrails of animals, clarified into something of pellucidity. All this Olaf, I hope, further perfected, as he did the placing of the court ladies, court officials, and the like; but I doubt if the luxury of a glass window were ever known to him, or a cup to drink from that was not made of metal or horn. In fact it is chiefly for his son's sake I mention him here; and with the son, too, I have little real concern, but only a kind of fantastic.

This son bears the name of Magnus *Barfod* (Barefoot, or Bareleg); and if you ask why so, the answer is: He was used to appear in the streets of Nidaros (Trondhjem) now and then in complete Scotch Highland dress. Authentic tartan plaid and philibeg, at that epoch,—to the wonder of Trondhjem and us! The truth is, he had a mighty fancy for those Hebrides and other Scotch possessions of his; and seeing England now quite impossible, eagerly speculated on some conquest in Ireland as next best. He did, in fact, go diligently voyaging and inspecting among those Orkney and Hebridian Isles; putting everything straight there, appointing stringent authorities, jarls,—nay, a king, "Kingdom of the Suderoer" (Southern Isles, now called *Sodor*),—and, as first king, Sigurd, his pretty little boy of nine years. All which done, and some quarrel with Sweden fought out, he seriously applied himself to visiting in a still more emphatic manner; namely, to invading, with his best skill and strength, the considerable virtual or actual kingdom he had in Ireland, intending fully to enlarge it to the utmost limits of the Island if possible. He got prosperously into Dublin (guess A.D. 1102). Considerable authority he already had, even among those poor Irish Kings, or kinglets, in their glibs and yellow–saffron gowns; still more, I suppose, among the numerous Norse Principalities there. "King Murdog, King of Ireland," says the Chronicle of Man, "had obliged himself, every Yule–day, to take a pair of shoes, hang them over his shoulder, as your servant does on a journey, and walk across his court, at bidding and in presence of Magnus Barefoot's messenger, by way of homage to the said "King." Murdog on this greater occasion did whatever homage could be required of him; but that, though comfortable, was far from satisfying the great King's ambitious mind. The great King left Murdog; left his own Dublin; marched off westward on a general conquest of Ireland. Marched easily victorious for a time; and got, some say, into the wilds of Connaught, but there saw himself beset by ambuscades and wild Irish countenances intent on mischief; and had, on the sudden, to draw up for battle;—place, I regret to say, altogether undiscoverable to me; known only that it was boggy in the extreme. Certain enough, too certain and evident, Magnus Barefoot, searching eagerly, could find no firm footing there; nor, fighting furiously up to the knees or deeper, any result but honorable death! Date is confidently marked "24 August, 1103,"—as if people knew the very day of the month. The natives did humanely give King Magnus Christian burial. The remnants of his force, without further molestation, found their ships on the Coast of Ulster; and sailed home,—without conquest of Ireland; nay perhaps, leaving royal Murdog disposed to be relieved of his procession with the pair of shoes.

Magnus Barefoot left three sons, all kings at once, reigning peaceably together. But to us, at present, the only noteworthy one of them was Sigurd; who, finding nothing special to do at home, left his brothers to manage for him, and went off on a far Voyage, which has rendered him distinguishable in the crowd. Voyage through the Straits of Gibraltar, on to Jerusalem, thence to Constantinople; and so home through Russia, shining with such renown as filled all Norway for the time being. A King called Sigurd Jorsalafarer (Jerusalemer) or Sigurd the Crusader henceforth. His voyage had been only partially of the Viking type; in general it was of the Royal–Progress kind rather; Vikingism only intervening in cases of incivility or the like. His reception in the Courts of Portugal, Spain, Sicily, Italy, had been honorable and sumptuous. The King of Jerusalem broke out into utmost splendor and effusion at sight of such a pilgrim; and Constantinople did its highest honors to such a Prince of Vaeringers. And the truth is, Sigurd intrinsically was a wise, able, and prudent man; who, surviving both his brothers, reigned a good while alone in a solid and successful way. He shows features of an original, independent–thinking man; something of ruggedly strong, sincere, and honest, with peculiarities that are amiable and even pathetic in the character and temperament of him; as certainly, the course of life he took was of his own choosing, and peculiar enough. He happens furthermore to be, what he least of all could have chosen or expected, the last of the Haarfagr Genealogy that had any success, or much deserved any, in this world. The last of the Haarfagrs, or as good as the last! So that, singular to say, it is in reality, for one thing only that Sigurd, after all his crusadings and wonderful adventures, is memorable to us here: the advent of an Irish gentleman called "Gylle Krist" (Gil–christ, Servant of Christ), who,—not over welcome, I should think, but (unconsciously) big with the above result,—appeared in Norway, while King Sigurd was supreme. Let us explain a little.

This Gylle Krist, the unconsciously fatal individual, who "spoke Norse imperfectly," declared himself to be the natural son of whilom Magnus Barefoot; born to him there while engaged in that unfortunate "Conquest of Ireland." "Here is my mother come with me," said Gilchrist, "who declares my real baptismal name to have been Harald, given me

71

by that great King; and who will carry the red–hot ploughshares or do any reasonable ordeal in testimony of these facts. I am King Sigurd's veritable half–brother: what will King Sigurd think it fair to do with me?" Sigurd clearly seems to have believed the man to be speaking truth; and indeed nobody to have doubted but he was. Sigurd said, "Honorable sustenance shalt thou have from me here. But, under pain of extirpation, swear that, neither in my time, nor in that of my young son Magnus, wilt thou ever claim any share in this Government." Gylle swore; and punctually kept his promise during Sigurd's reign. But during Magnus's, he conspicuously broke it; and, in result, through many reigns, and during three or four generations afterwards, produced unspeakable contentions, massacrings, confusions in the country he had adopted. There are reckoned, from the time of Sigurd's death (A.D. 1130), about a hundred years of civil war: no king allowed to distinguish himself by a solid reign of well–doing, or by any continuing reign at all,—sometimes as many as four kings simultaneously fighting;—and in Norway, from sire to son, nothing but sanguinary anarchy, disaster and bewilderment; a Country sinking steadily as if towards absolute ruin. Of all which frightful misery and discord Irish Gylle, styled afterwards King Harald Gylle, was, by ill destiny and otherwise, the visible origin: an illegitimate Irish Haarfagr who proved to be his own destruction, and that of the Haarfagr kindred altogether!

Sigurd himself seems always to have rather favored Gylle, who was a cheerful, shrewd, patient, witty, and effective fellow; and had at first much quizzing to endure, from the younger kind, on account of his Irish way of speaking Norse, and for other reasons. One evening, for example, while the drink was going round, Gylle mentioned that the Irish had a wonderful talent of swift running and that there were among them people who could keep up with the swiftest horse. At which, especially from young Magnus, there were peals of laughter; and a declaration from the latter that Gylle and he would have it tried to–morrow morning! Gylle in vain urged that he had not himself professed to be so swift a runner as to keep up with the Prince's horses; but only that there were men in Ireland who could. Magnus was positive; and, early next morning, Gylle had to be on the ground; and the race, naturally under heavy bet, actually went off. Gylle started parallel to Magnus's stirrup; ran like a very roe, and was clearly ahead at the goal. "Unfair," said Magnus; "thou must have had hold of my stirrup–leather, and helped thyself along; we must try it again." Gylle ran behind the horse this second time; then at the end, sprang forward; and again was fairly in ahead. "Thou must have held by the tail," said Magnus; "not by fair running was this possible; we must try a third time!" Gylle started ahead of Magnus and his horse, this third time; kept ahead with increasing distance, Magnus

72

galloping his very best; and reached the goal more palpably foremost than ever. So that Magnus had to pay his bet, and other damage and humiliation. And got from his father, who heard of it soon afterwards, scoffing rebuke as a silly fellow, who did not know the worth of men, but only the clothes and rank of them, and well deserved what he had got from Gylle. All the time King Sigurd lived, Gylle seems to have had good recognition and protection from that famous man; and, indeed, to have gained favor all round, by his quiet social demeanor and the qualities he showed.

CHAPTER XIII. MAGNUS THE BLIND, HARALD GYLLE, AND MUTUAL EXTINCTION OF THE HAARFAGRS.

On Sigurd the Crusader's death, Magnus naturally came to the throne; Gylle keeping silence and a cheerful face for the time. But it was not long till claim arose on Gylle's part, till war and fight arose between Magnus and him, till the skilful, popular, ever-active and shifty Gylle had entirely beaten Magnus; put out his eyes, mutilated the poor body of him in a horrid and unnamable manner, and shut him up in a convent as out of the game henceforth. There in his dark misery Magnus lived now as a monk; called "Magnus the Blind" by those Norse populations; King Harald Gylle reigning victoriously in his stead. But this also was only for a time. There arose avenging kinsfolk of Magnus, who had no Irish accent in their Norse, and were themselves eager enough to bear rule in their native country. By one of these,—a terribly stronghanded, fighting, violent, and regardless fellow, who also was a Bastard of Magnus Barefoot's, and had been made a Priest, but liked it unbearably ill, and had broken loose from it into the wildest courses at home and abroad; so that his current name got to be "Slembi-diakn," Slim or Ill Deacon, under which he is much noised of in Snorro and the Sagas: by this Slim-Deacon, Gylle was put an end to (murdered by night, drunk in his sleep); and poor blind Magnus was brought out, and again set to act as King, or King's Cloak, in hopes Gylle's posterity would never rise to victory more. But Gylle's posterity did, to victory and also to defeat, and were the death of Magnus and of Slim-Deacon too, in a frightful way; and all got their own death by and by in a ditto. In brief, these two kindreds (reckoned to be authentic enough Haarfagr people, both kinds of them) proved now to have become a veritable crop of dragon's teeth; who mutually fought, plotted, struggled, as if it had been their life's business; never ended fighting and seldom long intermitted it, till they had exterminated one another, and did at last all rest in death. One of these later Gylle temporary Kings I remember by the name of Harald Herdebred, Harald of the Broad

Shoulders. The very last of them I think was Harald Mund (Harald of the *Wry–Mouth*), who gave rise to two Impostors, pretending to be Sons of his, a good while after the poor Wry–Mouth itself and all its troublesome belongings were quietly underground. What Norway suffered during that sad century may be imagined.

CHAPTER XIV. SVERRIR AND DESCENDANTS, TO HAKON THE OLD.

The end of it was, or rather the first abatement, and *beginnings* of the end, That, when all this had gone on ever worsening for some forty years or so, one Sverrir (A.D. 1177), at the head of an armed mob of poor people called *Birkebeins*, came upon the scene. A strange enough figure in History, this Sverrir and his Birkebeins! At first a mere mockery and dismal laughing–stock to the enlightened Norway public. Nevertheless by unheard–of fighting, hungering, exertion, and endurance, Sverrir, after ten years of such a death–wrestle against men and things, got himself accepted as King; and by wonderful expenditure of ingenuity, common cunning, unctuous Parliamentary Eloquence or almost Popular Preaching, and (it must be owned) general human faculty and valor (or value) in the over–clouded and distorted state, did victoriously continue such. And founded a new Dynasty in Norway, which ended only with Norway's separate existence, after near three hundred years.

This Sverrir called himself a Son of Harald Wry–Mouth; but was in reality the son of a poor Comb–maker in some little town of Norway; nothing heard of Sonship to Wry–Mouth till after good success otherwise. His Birkebeins (that is to say, *Birchlegs;* the poor rebellious wretches having taken to the woods; and been obliged, besides their intolerable scarcity of food, to thatch their bodies from the cold with whatever covering could be got, and their legs especially with birch bark; sad species of fleecy hosiery; whence their nickname),—his Birkebeins I guess always to have been a kind of Norse *Jacquerie*: desperate rising of thralls and indigent people, driven mad by their unendurable sufferings and famishings,—theirs the deepest stratum of misery, and the densest and heaviest, in this the general misery of Norway, which had lasted towards the third generation and looked as if it would last forever:—whereupon they had risen proclaiming, in this furious dumb manner, unintelligible except to Heaven, that the same could not, nor would not, be endured any longer! And, by their Sverrir, strange to say, they did attain a kind of permanent success; and, from being a dismal laughing–stock in

74

Norway, came to be important, and for a time all—important there. Their opposition nicknames, "Baglers (from Bagall, *baculus*, bishop's staff; Bishop Nicholas being chief Leader)," "Gold—legs," and the like obscure terms (for there was still a considerable course of counter—fighting ahead, and especially of counter—nicknaming), I take to have meant in Norse prefigurement seven centuries ago, "bloated Aristocracy," "tyrannous—Bourgeoisie,"—till, in the next century, these rents were closed again!

King Sverrir, not himself bred to comb—making, had, in his fifth year, gone to an uncle, Bishop in the Faroe Islands; and got some considerable education from him, with a view to Priesthood on the part of Sverrir. But, not liking that career, Sverrir had fled and smuggled himself over to the Birkebeins; who, noticing the learned tongue, and other miraculous qualities of the man, proposed to make him Captain of them; and even threatened to kill him if he would not accept,—which thus at the sword's point, as Sverrir says, he was obliged to do. It was after this that he thought of becoming son of Wry—Mouth and other higher things.

His Birkebeins and he had certainly a talent of campaigning which has hardly ever been equalled. They fought like devils against any odds of number; and before battle they have been known to march six days together without food, except, perhaps, the inner barks of trees, and in such clothing and shoeing as mere birch bark:—at one time, somewhere in the Dovrefjeld, there was serious counsel held among them whether they should not all, as one man, leap down into the frozen gulfs and precipices, or at once massacre one another wholly, and so finish. Of their conduct in battle, fiercer than that of *Baresarks*, where was there ever seen the parallel? In truth they are a dim strange object to one, in that black time; wondrously bringing light into it withal; and proved to be, under such unexpected circumstances, the beginning of better days!

Of Sverrir's public speeches there still exist authentic specimens; wonderful indeed, and much characteristic of such a Sverrir. A comb—maker King, evidently meaning several good and solid things; and effecting them too, athwart such an element of Norwegian chaos—come—again. His descendants and successors were a comparatively respectable kin. The last and greatest of them I shall mention is Hakon VII., or Hakon the Old; whose fame is still lively among us, from the Battle of Largs at least.

CHAPTER XV. HAKON THE OLD AT LARGS.

In the Norse annals our famous Battle of Largs makes small figure, or almost none at all among Hakon's battles and feats. They do say indeed, these Norse annalists, that the King of Scotland, Alexander III. (who had such a fate among the crags about Kinghorn in time coming), was very anxious to purchase from King Hakon his sovereignty of the Western Isles, but that Hakon pointedly refused; and at length, being again importuned and bothered on the business, decided on giving a refusal that could not be mistaken. Decided, namely, to go with a big expedition, and look thoroughly into that wing of his Dominions; where no doubt much has fallen awry since Magnus Barefoot's grand visit thither, and seems to be inviting the cupidity of bad neighbors! "All this we will put right again," thinks Hakon, "and gird it up into a safe and defensive posture." Hakon sailed accordingly, with a strong fleet; adjusting and rectifying among his Hebrides as he went long, and landing withal on the Scotch coast to plunder and punish as he thought fit. The Scots say he had claimed of them Arran, Bute, and the Two Cumbraes ("given my ancestors by Donald Bain," said Hakon, to the amazement of the Scots) "as part of the Sudoer" (Southern Isles): —so far from selling that fine kingdom!—and that it was after taking both Arran and Bute that he made his descent at Largs.

Of Largs there is no mention whatever in Norse books. But beyond any doubt, such is the other evidence, Hakon did land there; land and fight, not conquering, probably rather beaten; and very certainly "retiring to his ships," as in either case he behooved to do! It is further certain he was dreadfully maltreated by the weather on those wild coasts; and altogether credible, as the Scotch records bear, that he was so at Largs very specially. The Norse Records or Sagas say merely, he lost many of his ships by the tempests, and many of his men by land fighting in various parts,—tacitly including Largs, no doubt, which was the last of these misfortunes to him. "In the battle here he lost 15,000 men, say the Scots, we 5,000"! Divide these numbers by ten, and the excellently brief and lucid Scottish summary by Buchanan may be taken as the approximately true and exact.[19] Date of the battle is A.D. 1263.

To this day, on a little plain to the south of the village, now town, of Largs, in Ayrshire, there are seen stone cairns and monumental heaps, and, until within a century ago, one huge, solitary, upright stone; still mutely testifying to a battle there,—altogether clearly, to this battle of King Hakon's; who by the Norse records, too, was in these neighborhoods at that same date, and evidently in an aggressive, high kind of humor. For "while his ships and army were doubling the Mull of Cantire, he had his own boat set on wheels, and therein, splendidly enough, had himself drawn across the Promontory at a flatter part," no doubt with horns sounding, banners waving. "All to the left of me is mine and Norway's," exclaimed Hakon in his triumphant boat progress, which such disasters soon followed.

Hakon gathered his wrecks together, and sorrowfully made for Orkney. It is possible enough, as our Guide Books now say, he may have gone by Iona, Mull, and the narrow seas inside of Skye; and that the Kyle–Akin, favorably known to sea–bathers in that region, may actually mean the Kyle (narrow strait) of Hakon, where Hakon may have dropped anchor, and rested for a little while in smooth water and beautiful environment, safe from equinoctial storms. But poor Hakon's heart was now broken. He went to Orkney; died there in the winter; never beholding Norway more.

He it was who got Iceland, which had been a Republic for four centuries, united to his kingdom of Norway: a long and intricate operation,—much presided over by our Snorro Sturleson, so often quoted here, who indeed lost his life (by assassination from his sons–in–law) and out of great wealth sank at once into poverty of zero,—one midnight in his own cellar, in the course of that bad business. Hakon was a great Politician in his time; and succeeded in many things before he lost Largs. Snorro's death by murder had happened about twenty years before Hakon's by broken heart. He is called Hakon the Old, though one finds his age was but fifty–nine, probably a longish life for a Norway King. Snorro's narrative ceases when Snorro himself was born; that is to say, at the threshold of King Sverrir; of whose exploits and doubtful birth it is guessed by some that Snorro willingly forbore to speak in the hearing of such a Hakon.

CHAPTER XVI. EPILOGUE.

Haarfagr's kindred lasted some three centuries in Norway; Sverrir's lasted into its third century there; how long after this, among the neighboring kinships, I did not inquire. For, by regal affinities, consanguinities, and unexpected chances and changes, the three Scandinavian kingdoms fell all peaceably together under Queen Margaret, of the Calmar Union (A.D. 1397); and Norway, incorporated now with Denmark, needed no more kings.

The History of these Haarfagrs has awakened in me many thoughts: Of Despotism and Democracy, arbitrary government by one and self–government (which means no government, or anarchy) by all; of Dictatorship with many faults, and Universal Suffrage with little possibility of any virtue. For the contrast between Olaf Tryggveson, and a Universal–Suffrage Parliament or an "Imperial" Copper Captain has, in these nine centuries, grown to be very great. And the eternal Providence that guides all this, and produces alike these entities with their epochs, is not its course still through the great deep? Does not it still speak to us, if we have ears? Here, clothed in stormy enough passions and instincts, unconscious of any aim but their own satisfaction, is the blessed beginning of Human Order, Regulation, and real Government; there, clothed in a highly different, but again suitable garniture of passions, instincts, and equally unconscious as to real aim, is the accursed–looking ending (temporary ending) of Order, Regulation, and Government;—very dismal to the sane onlooker for the time being; not dismal to him otherwise, his hope, too, being steadfast! But here, at any rate, in this poor Norse theatre, one looks with interest on the first transformation, so mysterious and abstruse, of human Chaos into something of articulate Cosmos; witnesses the wild and strange birth–pangs of Human Society, and reflects that without something similar (little as men expect such now), no Cosmos of human society ever was got into existence, nor can ever again be.

The violences, fightings, crimes—ah yes, these seldom fail, and they are very lamentable. But always, too, among those old populations, there was one saving element; the now want of which, especially the unlamented want, transcends all lamentation. Here is one of those strange, piercing, winged–words of Ruskin, which has in it a terrible truth for us in these epochs now come:—

"My friends, the follies of modern Liberalism, many and great though they be, are practically summed in this denial or neglect of the quality and intrinsic value of things. Its rectangular beatitudes, and spherical benevolences,—theology of universal indulgence, and jurisprudence which will hang no rogues, mean, one and all of them, in the root, incapacity of discerning, or refusal to discern, worth and unworth in anything, and least of all in man; whereas Nature and Heaven command you, at your peril, to discern worth from unworth in everything, and most of all in man. Your main problem is that ancient and trite one, 'Who is best man?' and the Fates forgive much,—forgive the wildest, fiercest, cruelest experiments,—if fairly made for the determination of that.

Theft and blood–guiltiness are not pleasing in their sight; yet the favoring powers of the spiritual and material world will confirm to you your stolen goods, and their noblest voices applaud the lifting of Your spear, and rehearse the sculpture of your shield, if only your robbing and slaying have been in fair arbitrament of that question, 'Who is best man?' But if you refuse such inquiry, and maintain every man for his neighbor's match,—if you give vote to the simple and liberty to the vile, the powers of those spiritual and material worlds in due time present you inevitably with the same problem, soluble now only wrong side upwards; and your robbing and slaying must be done then to find out, 'Who is worst man?' Which, in so wide an order of merit, is, indeed, not easy; but a complete Tammany Ring, and lowest circle in the Inferno of Worst, you are sure to find, and to be governed by."[20]

All readers will admit that there was something naturally royal in these Haarfagr Kings. A wildly great kind of kindred; counts in it two Heroes of a high, or almost highest, type: the first two Olafs, Tryggveson and the Saint. And the view of them, withal, as we chance to have it, I have often thought, how essentially Homeric it was:—indeed what is "Homer" himself but the *Rhapsody* of five centuries of Greek Skalds and wandering Ballad–singers, done (i.e. "stitched together") by somebody more musical than Snorro was? Olaf Tryggveson and Olaf Saint please me quite as well in their prosaic form; offering me the truth of them as if seen in their real lineaments by some marvellous opening (through the art of Snorro) across the black strata of the ages. Two high, almost among the highest sons of Nature, seen as they veritably were; fairly comparable or superior to god–like Achilleus, goddess–wounding Diomedes, much more to the two Atreidai, Regulators of the Peoples.

I have also thought often what a Book might be made of Snorro, did there but arise a man furnished with due literary insight, and indefatigable diligence; who, faithfully acquainting himself with the topography, the monumental relies and illustrative actualities of Norway, carefully scanning the best testimonies as to place and time which that country can still give him, carefully the best collateral records and chronologies of other countries, and who, himself possessing the highest faculty of a Poet, could, abridging, arranging, elucidating, reduce Snorro to a polished Cosmic state, unweariedly purging away his much chaotic matter! A modern "highest kind of Poet," capable of unlimited slavish labor withal;—who, I fear, is not soon to be expected in this world, or likely to find his task in the Heimskringla if he did appear here.

F   o   o   t   n   o   t   e   s   :

---

[1] J. G. Dahlmann, *Geschichte von Dannemark*, 3 vols. 8vo. Hamburg, 1840–1843.

[2] "Settlement," dated 912, by Munch, Henault, The Saxon Chronicle says (anno 876): "In this year Rolf overran Normandy with his army, and he reigned fifty winters."

[3] Dahlmann, ii. 87.

[4] Dahlmann, ii. 93.

[5] *Laing's Snorro*, i. 344.

[6] G. Buchanani *Opera Omnia*, i. 103, 104 (Curante Ruddimano, Edinburgi, 1715).

[7] His Long Serpent, judged by some to be of the size of a frigate of forty–five guns (Laing).

[8] This sermon was printed by Hearne; and is given also by Langebek in his excellent Collection, *Rerum Danicarum Scriptores Medii AEri*. Hafniae. 1772–1834.

[9] Kennet, i. 67; Rapin, i. 119, 121 (from the *Saxon Chronicle* both).

[10] Knut born A.D. 988 according to Munch's calculation (ii. 126).

[11] Snorro, Laing's Translation, ii. p. 31 et seq., will minutely specify.

[12] Snorro, ii. pp. 24, 25.

[13] Snorro, ii. pp. 156–161.

[14] Snorro, ii. pp. 252, 253.

[15] *Saxon Chronicle* says expressly, under A.D. 1030: "In this year King Olaf was slain in Norway by his own people, and was afterwards sainted."

[16] *Saxon Chronicle* says: "1035. In this year died King Cnut. ... He departed at Shaftesbury, November 12, and they conveyed him thence to Winchester, and there buried him."

[17] Munch gives the date 1038 (ii. 840), Adam of Bremen 1040.

[18] Camden, Rapin, quote.

[19] *Buchanani Hist.* i. 130.

[20] *Fors Clavigera*, Letter XIV. Pp. 8–10.

Printed in the United States
30994LVS00001BA/60

9 781419 117121